Ideas for
ENTERTAINING

Member Recipes

Minnetonka, Minnesota

Ideas for Entertaining—Member Recipes

Printed in 2006.

Tom Carpenter
Creative Director

Jen Weaverling
Production Editor

Kate Opseth
Graphic Designer

Steve Foley
Book Production

Mark Macemon
Commissoned Photography

Michelle Joy
Prop Stylist

Susan Brosious
Food Stylist

Jerry Dudycha
Assistant Food Stylist

Special thanks to: Terry Casey, Janice Cauley, Lori Grosklags, Nancy Maurer, Ruth Petran and Elaine Winch.

Special Note: The Cooking Club of America proudly presents this special cookbook edition which includes the personal favorites of your fellow members. Each recipe has been screened by a cooking professional and edited for clarity. However, we are not able to kitchen-test these recipes and cannot guarantee their outcome, or your safety in their preparation or consumption. Please be advised that any recipes which require the use of dangerous equipment (such as pressure cookers) or potentially unsafe preparation procedures (such as canning and pickling) should be used with caution and safe, healthy practices.

1 2 3 4 5 6 7 8 9 10 / 10 09 08 07 06
© 2006 Cooking Club of America
ISBN 10: 1-58159-278-7
ISBN 13: 978-1-58159-278-8

Cooking Club of America
12301 Whitewater Drive
Minnetonka, MN 55343
www.cookingclub.com

CONTENTS

From an intimate dinner party to an all-out bash, look to these

Ideas for Entertaining

the next time you're having guests over!

In one form or another, most Cooking Club of America Members enjoy the entire process of entertaining friends or family at home. It's always fun to plan, shop, prepare, cook, gather, relax, visit, socialize ... and eat!

In fact, eating is usually *the* focal point of any home-based gathering. So you want to make something great. It's a chance to show off your culinary skills, draw rave reviews, and feel an enormous sense of satisfaction as guests devour your creations and come back for more.

That's where this book, *Ideas for Entertaining,* comes in. Here are almost 300 recipes directly from fellow Cooking Club of America Members. These are Members' top-notch, all-time-favorite recipes for special occasions of all kinds.

The concepts here run a wide and delightful gamut.

You'll find *Appetizers and Starters* galore. *Salads and Sides* brings you dozens of ideas to accent your meals perfectly. *Soups and Sandwiches* give you plenty of casual creations for low-key gatherings. And *Slow Cooker Meals* let you keep busy on other projects as dinner takes care of itself.

The *Main Attractions* chapter features an eclectic mix of some of the best entrees you will ever find. *One Dish Meals* shows you how to cook simple yet fantastic-tasting creations in but one pan. And *Special Creations* introduces you to dozens of all-new ideas you're going to love creating and serving.

And don't forget dessert! Between *Delightful Desserts* and *Dessert Traditions,* you have many beautiful and tastefully-sweet options to choose from. Don't settle for store-bought dessert when you can make something awesome on your own.

One final thought: Don't restrict yourself to just special occasions with these recipes. There are plenty of concepts here that will work for "everyday" usage too. Why wait for the weekend to eat well?

You are holding one of the finest recipe collections we have ever seen. So enjoy being armed with plenty of *Ideas for Entertaining* that will keep you (and your guests) happy for years to come!

Appetizers
AND
Starters

ANTIPASTO SQUARES

Karen De Orio, Ellington, CT

2 (8-oz.) pkgs. refrigerated crescent rolls

¼ lb. thinly sliced Genoa salami

¼ lb. thinly sliced Swiss cheese

¼ lb. thinly sliced provolone cheese

¼ lb. thinly sliced pepperoni

¼ lb. thinly sliced ham

1 (12-oz.) jar roasted red bell peppers, drained

Freshly grated Parmesan cheese

Chopped fresh parsley

4 eggs, beaten

❶ Heat oven to 350°F. Spray 13x9-inch pan with cooking spray.

❷ Spread one package of the crescent rolls evenly into prepared pan. Top with salami, Swiss cheese, provolone cheese, pepperoni, ham and roasted peppers. Sprinkle with Parmesan cheese and parsley. Pour eggs over all, reserving a small amount. Cover with second package of crescent rolls; brush with remaining egg. Cover with aluminum foil. Bake 40 minutes; uncover and bake an additional 15 to 20 minutes.

24 servings.

ARTICHOKE HEART DIP

Jean Greenberg, Elk River, MN

1 (14-oz.) can artichoke hearts, drained, chopped

1 cup shredded mozzarella cheese

½ cup freshly grated Parmesan cheese

1 cup mayonnaise

1 teaspoon garlic, chopped, ready to use, or 1 to 2 garlic cloves, minced

1 teaspoon chopped fresh parsley

❶ Heat oven to 350°F.

❷ Thoroughly mix artichoke hearts, mozzarella cheese, Parmesan cheese, mayonnaise, garlic and parsley together in large bowl. Spread evenly into quiche dish or flat baking dish. Bake 25 minutes or until edges brown. Blot extra oil on top of dip with paper towels, if desired. Serve with crackers or bread.

24 to 32 servings.

ASPARAGUS BITES

Ann Stock, St. Charles, MO

20 slices white bread, crusts removed

3 oz. blue cheese, crumbled

8 oz. cream cheese, softened

1 egg

20 to 40 thin spears fresh asparagus, cooked, drained

½ lb. melted butter

❶ Heat oven to 400°F.

❷ Flatten trimmed bread with rolling pin. Stir together blue cheese, cream cheese and egg in medium bowl until combined. Spread over bread slices. Place 2 asparagus spears over cheese and roll up jelly roll style. Dip in melted butter and cut into 3 pieces. Bake on baking sheet 25 minutes or until lightly browned. If desired, bites can be made ahead and frozen.

60 bites.

DILL DIP

Cathy Miller, Hanover, PA

2 cups sour cream

2 cups mayonnaise

2 teaspoons Bon Appetit seasoning

2 tablespoons dried parsley

2 teaspoons dried dill

2 tablespoons minced onion

1 Mix sour cream, mayonnaise, Bon Appetit seasoning, parsley, dill and onion in large bowl; chill. Serve with vegetables, pretzels, in a bread bowl, or on a salad.

Servings vary.

BEER BATTER HALIBUT APPETIZERS

Gena Stout, Ravenden, AR

1½ cups buttermilk pancake mix

2 tablespoons cornmeal

½ teaspoon salt

¼ teaspoon onion powder

¼ teaspoon garlic powder

¼ teaspoon dry mustard

⅛ teaspoon freshly ground pepper

¾ cup beer

1½ lbs. halibut fillet, cut in 1-inch pieces

Oil for deep frying

1 Heat oil to 375°F in deep fryer.

2 Combine ⅓ cup pancake mix, cornmeal, salt, onion powder, garlic powder, mustard and pepper in large shallow bowl. Set aside. Gradually add beer to remaining pancake mix in large shallow bowl. Stir to combine. Dip halibut pieces in dry ingredients to coat, then in beer batter. Fry halibut, a few pieces at a time until crisp and golden, about 2 minutes.

3 dozen.

CHEESE BALLS

Jolynn Spinelli, Honolulu, HI

½ cup unsalted butter, softened

1 cup shredded sharp cheddar cheese

1¼ cups all-purpose flour

½ teaspoon salt

½ teaspoon sweet paprika

¼ teaspoon cayenne pepper

1 Heat over to 400°F.

2 In medium bowl, cream together butter and cheese. In separate medium bowl, whisk together flour, salt, paprika and cayenne pepper. Add dry ingredients to cheese mixture and knead until soft dough forms, approximately 3 to 4 minutes.

3 Working quickly, roll a piece of dough, roughly tablespoon sized, between hands to form a ball. Place cheese balls on parchment-lined baking sheet 1 inch apart. Bake 12 minutes or until puffed and golden.

24 to 32 servings.

TACO DIP

Abby Wilson, Chanhassen, MN

2 (8-oz.) pkgs. cream cheese, softened

1 (16-oz.) jar salsa, drained

1 lb. shredded cheddar cheese

1 Spread softened cream cheese on bottom of shallow baking dish. Top with salsa and cheddar cheese. Microwave on high 5 to 8 minutes or until cheese is melted. Let stand 10 minutes. Serve with chips or crackers.

SWEET-N-SOUR MEATBALLS

Cindy Sasek, Webb City, MO

SAUCE

2 cups ketchup

½ cup chopped onion

½ teaspoon garlic powder

2 teaspoons liquid smoke

2 cups packed brown sugar

½ can beer

MEATBALLS

3 lbs. ground beef

1 (12-oz.) can evaporated milk

2 cups coarsely crushed crackers

1 medium onion, chopped

2 eggs

½ teaspoon garlic powder

½ teaspoon freshly ground pepper

2 teaspoons salt

❶ Heat oven to 350°F.

❷ For Sauce: Mix ketchup, onion, garlic powder, liquid smoke, brown sugar and beer in large saucepan; bring mixture to a boil, stirring constantly.

❸ For Meatballs: Mix ground beef, evaporated milk, crackers, onion, eggs, garlic powder, pepper and salt in large bowl; shape into balls and place in 13x9-inch pan. Cover with sauce; bake 1 hour until no longer pink in center.

Servings vary.

CAPRESE BITES

Jodi Paige Walker, Tucson, AZ

1 bunch fresh basil

1 small container fresh mozzarella balls, drained

1 container cherry tomatoes, halved

Balsamic vinegar, to taste

Extra-virgin olive oil, to taste

❶ Stack a basil leaf, mozzarella ball and tomato half and secure with toothpick, wrapping basil around mozzarella ball and tomato half if basil leaves are large enough. Continue with remaining ingredients. Place on serving platter and sprinkle lightly with balsamic vinegar and extra-virgin olive oil.

24 to 32 servings.

TIO MIGUEL'S SALSA PICANTE FRESCA

Mike Hastie, Austin, TX

3 (14.5-oz.) cans stewed tomatoes

1 onion, chopped

4 to 6 garlic cloves, minced

5 to 8 large fresh jalapeño chiles

6 to 8 large Serrano chiles

1 teaspoon dried oregano

1½ teaspoons Comino (cumin)

Juice of 1½ limes

Sea salt or kosher (coarse) salt, to taste

Fresh cilantro, to taste

2 teaspoons ketchup

Dash chipotle sauce

❶ In blender or food processor, layer tomatoes, onion, garlic, three-quarters of the chiles, oregano, Comino, lime juice, salt, cilantro, ketchup and chipotle sauce. Pulse to combine. Add more chiles if desired and continue pulsing to combine. Add 2 or 3 canned chipotle chiles for a rich hot smoky flavor, if desired.

Servings vary.

Caprese Bites

CHRIS'S SEAFOOD DIP

Christina Mendoza, Alamogordo, NM

½ cup shredded Italian cheese blend

4 oz. cream cheese, softened

½ oz. creamy Brie cheese

½ cup sour cream

1 (4-oz.) can tiny shrimp or crabmeat, drained

¼ to ½ teaspoon minced garlic

6 oz. chopped marinated artichokes

Freeze-dried chives, to taste

2 tablespoons dry sherry

½ teaspoon white wine Worcestershire sauce, if desired

½ to 1 bunch green onions, sliced

Paprika, to taste

Round bread loaf, if desired

1 Heat oven to 375°F.

2 In medium bowl, stir together cheese blend, cream cheese, Brie cheese, sour cream, shrimp, garlic, artichokes, chives, sherry, Worcestershire sauce and onions. Place mixture in ovenproof 2- to 3-quart pan or hollowed out bread bowl. Sprinkle paprika on top. Bake 20 to 30 minutes or until browned and bubbly.

Servings vary.

CHICKEN AND CHEESE NACHOS

Cindy Logsdon, Joplin, MO

1½ cups shredded Colby Monterey Jack cheese

1 (4-oz.) can chopped green chiles

1 (2¼-oz.) can sliced black olives, drained

¼ cup sliced green onion

¾ cup ranch dressing

½ cup medium salsa

2 boneless skinless chicken breast halves, cooked and shredded

36 to 40 round tortilla chips

1 Heat oven to 350°F.

2 In large bowl, combine cheese, peppers, olives, green onion, dressing and salsa. Fold in chicken. Arrange tortilla chips on a large baking sheet. Top each chip with a rounded teaspoon of mixture. Bake 10 minutes or until cheese melts. Serve warm.

6 servings.

CHOPPED EGGPLANT APPETIZER

Ann Miller, Amory, MS

1 large eggplant, halved

1 green or red bell pepper, halved

½ onion, chopped

2 tablespoons white vinegar

Freshly ground pepper, to taste

Salt, to taste

1 Heat oven to 425°F.

2 Pierce eggplant and bake eggplant and pepper on foil-lined baking sheet about 25 to 30 minutes until softened. Place in paper or plastic bag until cooled. Peel skins. Place all ingredients in food processor; pulse until chopped and mixed.

Servings vary.

CREAMY CRAB/SHRIMP SALAD

Brenda Waycaster, Murfreesboro, TN

1 (8-oz.) pkg. pre-cooked salad shrimp

4 oz. cream cheese, softened

¼ cup finely diced celery

¼ cup finely diced sweet or red onion

1 teaspoon lemon juice

1 teaspoon Worcestershire sauce

1 teaspoon prepared horseradish, if desired

½ teaspoon garlic powder

1 to 2 tablespoons mayonnaise

8 oz. flaked blue crab meat or imitation crabmeat, chopped

1 In medium bowl, mix together salad shrimp, cream cheese, celery, onion, lemon juice, Worcestershire sauce, horseradish and garlic powder until well blended. Add mayonnaise; stir to combine and gently fold in crabmeat. Add additional mayonnaise until mixture reaches the desired consistency. Serve on crackers or toasted rye bread cut into triangles or fry flour tortillas in oil and sprinkle with garlic salt; top with crab salad.

Servings vary.

FOOTBALL BITES

Mandy Nall, Lowndesboro, AL

50 cherry or 10 Roma tomatoes

¾ cup sour cream

1 cup mayonnaise

1 medium onion, finely chopped

½ cup finely shredded cheddar cheese

Lettuce leaves

Real bacon bits, warmed

1 Slice off top of tomatoes and remove seeds to form a cup. Stir together sour cream, mayonnaise and onion in medium bowl. Spoon mixture into tomatoes; sprinkle with cheese. Serve on lettuce leaves. Refrigerate at least 30 minutes. Top with warm bacon bits.

Servings vary.

STUFFED JALAPEÑO

Lisa Wentworth, Tucson, AZ

1 pkg. pork sausage (such as Jimmy Dean)

1 (8-oz.) pkg. cream cheese, softened

1 can whole pickled jalapeños, drained

2 lemons

Paprika, if desired

1 Brown sausage in large skillet until cooked and crumbly; drain.

2 In medium bowl, stir together sausage and cream cheese until combined. Cut the jalapeños lengthwise and discard seeds.

3 Fill large bowl half full with cold water and ice; squeeze in juice from lemons. Place jalapeño halves in the water and soak for 15 minutes. Remove and place on paper towels cut-side down; dry completely.

4 Generously fill jalapeños with the cream cheese mixture. Place on serving platter. Sprinkle with paprika, if desired. Refrigerate 1 hour or overnight.

Servings vary.

FRANKS IN SAUCE

Daniel McCarron, Lake Wales, FL

SAUCE

2 tablespoons vinegar

2 tablespoons lemon juice

2 tablespoons packed brown sugar

$\frac{1}{8}$ teaspoon cayenne pepper

1 cup ketchup

3 tablespoons Worcestershire sauce

$\frac{1}{2}$ tablespoon dry mustard

FRANKS

2 tablespoons shortening or vegetable oil

1 lb. cocktail franks or wieners

1 Combine vinegar, lemon juice, brown sugar, cayenne pepper, ketchup, Worcestershire sauce and dry mustard in large bowl.

2 Melt shortening in large skillet over medium heat. Add franks and brown on all sides. Pour in sauce; bring to a simmer and continue cooking about 20 minutes or until heated through.

8 to 10 servings.

CRAB SPREAD

Kathleen Hritz, Grafton, OH

1 (12- to 16-oz.) pkg. imitation crabmeat, cut up

$\frac{1}{4}$ cup mayonnaise

1 teaspoon prepared horseradish

2 to 3 tablespoons sliced green onions

1 (8-oz.) pkg. cream cheese, softened

2 tablespoons ketchup

1 Mix together crabmeat, mayonnaise, horseradish, onions, cream cheese and ketchup in large bowl and refrigerate until serving. Serve with crackers.

Servings vary.

FRUITED CHEESE BALL

Jill Wright, Dixon, IL

8 oz. cream cheese, softened

2 tablespoons butter, melted, cooled

1 teaspoon Worcestershire sauce

$\frac{1}{4}$ teaspoon garlic powder

$\frac{3}{4}$ cup shredded cheddar cheese

$\frac{3}{4}$ cup shredded Italian cheese blend (mozzarella, Romano and Parmesan)

2 green onions, sliced

1 (2-oz.) jar diced pimiento, drained

$\frac{1}{3}$ cup dried apricots, softened in boiling water, cooled, chopped

$\frac{1}{3}$ to $\frac{1}{2}$ cup finely chopped pecans

1 Beat together cream cheese, butter, Worcestershire and garlic powder in large bowl until fluffy. Stir in cheeses, onion, pimiento and apricots; blend well. Cover and chill until firm, at least 1 hour. Shape mixture into a ball and roll in pecans. Wrap in plastic wrap; refrigerate overnight.

24 to 32 servings.

WHITE CHOCOLATE MOUSSE DIP

Amber Shea Ford, Lawrence, KS

4 oz. cream cheese, softened

$1\frac{1}{2}$ cups cold milk

1 (4-serving size) pkg. white chocolate pudding mix

1 cup whipped topping

Dark chocolate shavings

1 Beat cream cheese and milk in medium bowl until well combined. Add pudding and beat until mixture is thickened, about 2 minutes. Gently fold in whipped topping. Refrigerate 1 hour. Garnish with dark chocolate shavings and serve with vanilla wafers, gingersnaps or animal crackers.

Servings vary.

HOT BLACK BEAN AND CORN DIP

Jennifer Okutman, Westminster, MD

1 (15-oz.) can black beans, drained and rinsed

1 (15-oz.) can whole kernel corn, drained

1 (10-oz.) can chopped tomatoes with jalapeño

1 teaspoon chili powder

1 teaspoon garlic powder

1 teaspoon ground cumin

Juice of ½ lime

Dash hot pepper sauce

1 (8-oz.) pkg. cream cheese, cubed

1 Heat oven to 350°F.

2 Combine beans, corn, tomatoes, spices, lime juice and hot sauce in large bowl. Gently fold in cream cheese. Pour bean mixture into 13x9-inch baking dish and bake 25 to 30 minutes. Serve with tortilla chips.

Servings vary.

LITTLE SMOKIES FINGERS

Carl Boutifier, Freeport, OH

1 (8-oz.) pkg. crescent rolls

Shredded cheese, to taste

Garlic powder, to taste

Onion powder, to taste

1 (16-oz.) pkg. Little Smokies wieners

1 Heat oven to 350°F.

2 Roll dough into 4 rectangles and firmly press seams together. Cut into squares. Sprinkle with shredded cheese, garlic and onion powder. Top with Smokies and roll up. Place on ungreased baking sheet and bake 10 to 12 minutes or until golden brown. If desired, sprinkle with assorted diced vegetables in place of the cheese.

2 dozen appetizers.

VEGGIE BAR RECIPE

Andrea Money, Knoxville, TN

2 (8-oz.) pkgs. crescent rolls

2 (8-oz.) pkgs. cream cheese

1 cup mayonnaise

1 (4-oz.) pkg. dry ranch dip mix

1 bunch broccoli

1 head cauliflower

1 to 2 tomatoes, chopped

1 pkg. shredded carrots

Assorted vegetables, to taste

2 cups shredded cheddar cheese

1 Roll crescents into 9x9-inch baking dish and bake according to package directions; cool.

2 Mix cream cheese, mayonnaise and dip mix together in a medium bowl; set aside.

3 Cut up broccoli, cauliflower and other veggies.

4 Spread cooled crescent rolls with cream cheese mixture. Top with shredded cheese and vegetables. Refrigerate until serving. Cut into squares.

Servings vary.

"Bloody Mary" Shrimp Cocktail

"BLOODY MARY" SHRIMP COCKTAIL

Brian Redman, Louisville, KY

SHRIMP

1 lb. fully cooked large shrimp

Juice of 1 lemon

SAUCE

1 (28-oz.) can crushed tomatoes

4 tablespoons vodka, if desired

Juice of $\frac{1}{2}$ lemon

1 rib celery, finely chopped

1 teaspoon freshly ground pepper

1 tablespoon prepared horseradish

2 tablespoons Worcestershire sauce

2 teaspoons hot pepper sauce

Fresh parsley sprigs

1 Place shrimp on large plate; squeeze lemon juice over the top. Mix crushed tomatoes, vodka, juice of $\frac{1}{2}$ lemon, celery, pepper, horseradish, Worcestershire sauce and hot pepper sauce together in large pitcher. Pour sauce into chilled martini glasses. Place 4 to 5 shrimp around sides of each glass. Garnish with parsley sprig.

6 to 8 servings.

HOT LOBSTER DIP

Barbara Mataronas, Little Compton, RI

1$\frac{1}{2}$ cups cooked fresh lobster meat, chopped

1 (8-oz.) pkg. cream cheese, softened

2 tablespoons milk

3 green onions, sliced

2 tablespoons prepared horseradish sauce

2 tablespoons mayonnaise

1 teaspoon hot pepper sauce

$\frac{1}{2}$ teaspoon dry mustard

3 tablespoons sweet vermouth, dry sherry, or milk

1 Mix lobster meat, cream cheese, milk, onions, horseradish sauce, mayonnaise, hot pepper sauce, mustard and vermouth in large bowl. Refrigerate at least 3 hours.

2 Heat oven to 350°F.

3 Spoon lobster mixture into 11x7-inch shallow baking dish. Bake 10 to 15 minutes or until heated through. Serve with crusty bread or crackers.

24 to 32 servings.

CHEESE BALL

Kathleen Hritz, Grafton, OH

8 oz. cream cheese, softened

4 oz. crumbled blue cheese

8 oz. shredded sharp or mild cheddar cheese

1 tablespoon Worcestershire sauce

$\frac{1}{4}$ cup chopped onion

1 Mix cream cheese, blue cheese, shredded cheese, Worcestershire sauce and chopped onion in large bowl. Shape into large ball. Serve with crackers.

Servings vary.

MEXICAN MARTINI

Margaret Elder, Gun Barrel City, TX

SAUCE

¾ cup white vinegar

½ cup sugar

5 garlic cloves, mashed

1 teaspoon salt

Juice of 1 small lime

6 plum tomatoes, chopped

¾ cup white onion, chopped

2 Serrano chiles, finely chopped

3 chipotle chiles in adobo sauce, coarsely chopped

1 yellow bell pepper, chopped

1 avocado, chopped

3 tablespoons chopped fresh cilantro

2 (8-oz.) pkgs. small cooked shrimp

½ cup tequila, if desired

1 Mix vinegar and sugar together in large bowl until sugar is dissolved. Add garlic cloves, salt and juice of lime.

2 In another large bowl, stir together tomatoes, onion, Serrano chiles, chipotle chiles, yellow pepper, avocado, cilantro and shrimp. Stir into sauce. Refrigerate overnight.

3 Just before serving stir in ½ cup tequila. Serve with tortilla chips.

Servings vary.

MINI SAUSAGE QUICHES

Pat Clevenger, Parma Heights, OH

½ cup butter, softened

3 oz. cream cheese, softened

1 cup all-purpose flour

½ lb. bulk Italian sausage

1 cup shredded Swiss cheese

1 tablespoon chopped fresh chives

2 eggs

1 cup half-and-half

¼ teaspoon salt

Dash cayenne pepper

1 Beat butter and cream cheese in medium bowl until creamy. Stir in flour; refrigerate 1 hour. Roll into 24 (1-inch) balls; press into mini muffin cups.

2 Heat oven to 375°F.

3 Cook sausage in medium skillet over medium-high heat until browned; drain. Sprinkle evenly into pastry shells; sprinkle with Swiss cheese and chives. Whisk eggs, half-and-half, salt and cayenne pepper in medium bowl until blended; pour over sausage. Bake 20 to 30 minutes or until set. Remove from pans. Serve hot.

24 appetizers.

LITTLE SMOKIES

Bonnie Woodward, Marco Island, FL

1 (16-oz.) pkg. Little Smokies wieners

1 lb. bacon, halved crosswise

1 cup packed brown sugar

1 Heat oven to 325°F.

2 Wrap each wiener with bacon; secure with toothpick. Place in a single layer on aluminum-foil-lined jelly roll pan. Sprinkle evenly with brown sugar. Bake 1½ hours and serve.

8 to 10 servings.

MUSHROOM BACON BITES

Susan Graves, Jonesboro, GA

1 (16-oz.) loaf square sliced sandwich bread

1 (10¾-oz.) can cream of mushroom soup

Bacon, cut into thirds

Cubed provolone or smoked Gouda cheese

Freshly grated Parmesan cheese, if desired

1 Heat oven to 375°F.

2 Spread each slice of bread with soup. Cut into thirds.

3 Place cheese cube in center and roll bread around the cheese. Wrap bacon around bread. Secure with toothpick. Bake until crisp and lightly brown. If desired, roll bacon-wrapped bread in Parmesan cheese before baking.

Servings vary.

SITTIN' ON A RITZ

Toni Pendley, Somerset, KY

1 (10-oz.) box chopped dates

1 (14-oz.) can sweetened condensed milk

1½ sleeves of buttery flavored round crackers

3 oz. white chocolate, chopped

1 Heat oven to 350°F.

2 Place chopped dates and milk in medium skillet and cook over low heat until dates dissolve, stirring constantly. Spread mixture on crackers and place on ungreased baking sheets. Bake 5 minutes.

3 Place white chocolate in large measuring cup and microwave on medium-high 2 minutes, stirring at 30-second intervals until melted. Top the crackers with melted chocolate; cool.

4 Store in an airtight container until ready to serve.

36 to 48 crackers.

OLIVE NUT SPREAD

Shirley Mattox, Buckeye, AZ

8 oz. cream cheese, softened

2 tablespoons salad dressing

½ cup chopped pecans

1 cup sliced green olives

2 tablespoons olive juice from jar

Dash freshly ground pepper

1 Beat cream cheese in large bowl on medium speed until fluffy; add salad dressing, pecans, olives, olive juice and pepper and beat until combined. Refrigerate overnight.

16 to 24 servings.

PARMESAN CHICKEN WINGS

Peggy M. Yamaguchi-Lazar, Eugene, OR

16 whole chicken wings

¾ cup finely crushed butter-flavored crackers

¾ cup freshly grated Parmesan cheese

1 teaspoon dried basil

¾ teaspoon garlic salt

¼ cup butter, melted

1 Heat oven to 375°F.

2 Cut chicken wings into three sections; discard wing tips.

3 In small bowl, combine cracker crumbs, Parmesan cheese, basil and garlic salt. Dip wings in butter, then roll in crumb mixture.

4 Place wings in a single layer on greased baking sheets. Bake 35 to 40 minutes or until golden brown and juices run clear.

8 to 10 servings.

PASTA PODS

Jodi Paige Walker, Tucson, AZ

1 cup diced Swiss cheese or cheese of choice

1 cup shredded carrots

1 cup diced green or red bell pepper

1 cup diced onion

1 cup diced pepperoni

1 cup canned garbanzo beans, rinsed and drained

1/4 cup Italian dressing

1 lb. large pasta shells, cooked

1 Toss Swiss cheese, carrots, green bell pepper, onion, pepperoni, garbanzo beans and Italian dressing in large bowl. Marinate for several hours or overnight. Spoon ingredients into cooked pasta shells. Arrange on serving platter.

8 to 10 servings.

POLISH DISASTERS

Joy Smrcina, Cleveland, OH

1 lb. ground sirloin

1 lb. hot pork sausage

2 lbs. processed cheese loaf

2 tablespoons Worcestershire sauce

1 (16-oz.) loaf party rye or pumpernickel bread

1 Heat oven to 350°F.

2 Brown sirloin and sausage together in large skillet; drain. Add cheese and Worcestershire sauce; cook until cheese is melted.

3 Place bread squares in single layer on baking sheets. Top bread with 1 to 2 tablespoons cheese mixture. Bake 5 to 7 minutes. Serve warm or room temperature. If desired, freeze for later use.

24 to 32 servings.

SUSIE'S FAMOUS CRANBERRY SALSA

Terri Hickey, Novato, CA

1 (12-oz.) bag cranberries

2 garlic cloves, minced

2 jalapeños, seeded if desired and chopped

2 green onions, thinly sliced

1/2 cup sugar

1/3 cup fresh lime juice, from 3 to 4 limes

Lime peel from above limes

Salt, to taste

Freshly ground pepper, to taste

1 Boil 1 quart of water in medium saucepan and add cranberries. Boil 1 minute or until cranberries pop. Drain; set aside.

2 Mix garlic, jalapeño and green onions in large bowl; stir in sugar, lime juice and cranberries. Coarsely mash cranberries, leaving most whole. Add lime peel, salt and pepper. Refrigerate 2 to 3 hours. Serve with turkey, chicken or with crackers.

Servings vary.

SPAM SPREAD

Lynn Diehl, Irving, TX

1 (12-oz.) can Spam

2 hard-boiled eggs

2 large or 3 small dill pickles

Finely chopped onion, to taste

Garlic salt, to taste

Mayonnaise, to taste

1 Grate spam, eggs and pickles into large bowl using a cheese grater; add the onion and garlic salt. Stir in mayonnaise, mixing until meat is moistened. Serve with buttery flavored crackers or use as sandwich filling.

Servings vary.

Susie's Famous Cranberry Salsa

SALMON PARTY LOG

Teresa McGrath, Porters Lake, NS, Canada

1 (1-lb.) can salmon, drained, bones removed, about 2 cups

1 (8-oz.) pkg. cream cheese, softened

1 tablespoon lemon juice

2 teaspoons grated onion

1 teaspoon prepared horseradish

¼ teaspoon salt

¼ teaspoon liquid smoke

½ cup chopped pecans

3 tablespoons chopped fresh parsley

❶ Flake salmon into medium bowl; add cream cheese, lemon juice, onion, horseradish, salt and liquid smoke. Combine pecans and parsley and spread evenly over waxed paper.

❷ Shape salmon mixture into 8x2-inch log. Roll the log in the pecan mixture. Chill until ready to serve. Serve with crackers.

12 to 16 servings.

OLIVE BALLS

Ann Stock, St. Charles, MO

1 cup all-purpose flour

⅔ cup softened butter

2 cups shredded cheddar cheese

Cayenne pepper, to taste

1 (12-oz.) jar pitted green olives, drained

❶ Heat oven to 400°F.

❷ Mix flour, butter, cheese and cayenne pepper in large bowl until a smooth dough is formed. Roll a piece of dough around each olive. Bake 15 minutes or until golden brown.

Servings vary.

SHRIMP APPETIZER PIZZA

Toni Pendley, Somerset, KY

1 (12-inch) pre-baked pizza crust

8 oz. cream cheese, softened

2 tablespoons skim milk

1 garlic clove, minced

½ teaspoon lemon-pepper seasoning

1 tablespoon dry Italian dressing mix, from a 1-oz pkg.

½ teaspoon dried oregano leaves, crushed

7 oz. salad shrimp, cooked

¼ cup diced red pepper

4 green onions, sliced

½ cup shredded cheddar cheese

½ cup shredded Pepper Jack cheese

❶ Heat oven to 350°F. Spray baking sheet with cooking spray.

❷ Bake pizza crust 10 minutes; cool.

❸ In small bowl, mix cream cheese, skim milk, garlic, lemon-pepper, Italian dressing and oregano. Spread over cooled crust. Sprinkle shrimp, red pepper and onions over dressing; top with cheese. Chill 2 hours or overnight.

❹ Trim the crust into a large square and cut into small squares to serve. Cover tightly with plastic wrap and chill until ready to serve.

24 servings.

PORTOBELLOS STUFFED WITH COUNTRY HAM

Brian Redman, Louisville, KY

2 tablespoons olive oil

2 medium onions, halved, cut into thin slices

1 cup country-style ham, finely chopped

½ cup freshly shredded Parmesan cheese

4 portobello mushroom caps, cleaned, stems removed

1 Heat oven to 375°F. Spray baking sheet with cooking spray.

2 Heat oil in large skillet over medium heat. Add onions and cook until onions are tender, about 10 minutes. Lower heat and cook until onions are caramelized; stir in ham and ¼ cup cheese. Remove from heat.

3 Place mushrooms on prepared baking sheet. Stuff the mushroom caps with the ham mixture. Sprinkle with remaining cheese. Bake 15 minutes.

4 servings.

STICKY CHICKEN WINGS

Marion Kouleas, Aldergrove, BC, Canada

Orange juice, to cover chicken wings

4 teaspoons soy sauce

4 teaspoons vinegar

1 teaspoon cayenne pepper

1 teaspoon dry mustard

2 tablespoons sugar

Chicken wings

1 Mix orange juice, soy sauce, vinegar, cayenne pepper, dry mustard and sugar in large saucepan. Place wings in pan, making sure they are covered with the orange juice. Bring to a boil, turn chicken to coat well. Reduce heat to medium; simmer until liquid has evaporated, about 1 hour. Turn wings every 15 to 20 minutes to make sure they are coated with liquid.

Servings vary.

WONTON "BON JOVIES"

Debbie S. Borries, Effingham, IL

1 lb. bulk Italian sausage

1½ cups shredded cheddar cheese

1½ cups shredded Monterey Jack cheese

½ cup chopped black olives

½ cup chopped red or green bell peppers, if desired

1 cup ranch dressing

24 round or square wonton wrappers

1 Heat oven to 350°F. Spray miniature muffin pan with cooking spray.

2 Cook sausage in large skillet over medium-high heat until browned and crumbly; drain.

3 Combine sausage, cheeses, olives, peppers and salad dressing in large bowl; mix well.

4 Place wonton wrappers into prepared muffin pan. Spray wrappers lightly with cooking spray. Bake 5 minutes or until lightly browned. Fill approximately two thirds full and bake an additional 5 minutes or until cheese melts. Remove from pan; serve hot or cold.

24 servings.

SPINACH AND BACON DEVILED EGGS

Diane Lyon, Mercerville, NJ

2 dozen hard-boiled eggs, peeled, halved lengthwise

1 (10-oz.) pkg. frozen chopped spinach, thawed, drained, squeezed dry

½ cup mayonnaise

5 strips bacon, cooked crisp and crumbled or ¼ cup real bacon bits

5 tablespoons cider vinegar

3 tablespoons butter, softened

2 tablespoons sugar substitute or granulated sugar

Salt, to taste

Freshly ground pepper, to taste

Fresh Italian leaf parsley, if desired

Sliced pimiento-stuffed green olives, if desired

1 Scoop yolks into medium bowl. Place egg whites on large platter for serving.

2 Mash yolks with fork; add spinach, mayonnaise, bacon, cider vinegar, butter, sugar, salt and pepper and mix well.

3 Spoon yolk mixture into egg white halves. Top each with a piece of flat leaf parsley or a slice of pimiento-stuffed green olive; chill before serving.

48 servings.

TOMATO MOZZARELLA BITES

Patty Woodland, Manahawkin, NJ

4 tablespoons extra-virgin olive oil

2 large garlic cloves, crushed

Salt, to taste

Freshly ground pepper, to taste

10 large fresh basil leaves

20 small fresh mozzarella balls, halved

40 grape tomatoes

2 tablespoons balsamic vinegar

1 In small saucepan, heat oil over medium-high heat until hot. Add garlic and cook 30 seconds or until fragrant. Stir in salt and pepper and set aside.

2 Cut 7 basil leaves in half, then in thirds making 42 pieces; set aside. Chop remaining basil into small pieces and add to the warm oil, garlic mixture.

3 Place halved mozzarella balls onto toothpicks; add a small piece of basil and a grape tomato; repeat.

4 Place about 2 tablespoons of the oil mixture on a serving platter and top with filled toothpicks; drizzle with remaining oil mixture and sprinkle with balsamic vinegar.

Servings vary.

Salads
AND
Sides

ALMOND SALAD

Ann Stock, St. Charles, MO

SALAD

½ cup sliced almonds

2 tablespoons vegetable oil or butter

1 head romaine lettuce, chopped

2 cups shredded provolone cheese

1 bunch green onions, sliced

DRESSING

½ cup oil

¼ cup vinegar

2 tablespoons sugar

1 tablespoon chopped fresh parsley

1 teaspoon salt

Dash freshly ground pepper

Dash Tabasco sauce

1 Toast almonds in large skillet in 2 tablespoons oil or butter until golden.

2 In large bowl mix lettuce, cheese, green onions and almonds.

3 Combine oil, vinegar, sugar, parsley, salt, pepper and Tabasco sauce in medium bowl; pour over salad to serve.

6 to 8 servings.

BEAN SALAD

Dzhangirova Sveteana, Seattle, WA

1 cup dried navy or kidney beans

4 tablespoons olive oil

1 large red onion, thinly sliced

½ cup dried cranberries

½ cup chopped walnuts

3 garlic cloves, minced

4 tablespoons chopped fresh cilantro

½ teaspoon ground coriander, if desired

Salt, to taste

Freshly ground pepper, to taste

1 Place beans in large saucepan and cover with cold water. Bring to a boil over medium-high heat; boil 3 minutes. Remove from heat; cover and let stand 1 hour. Drain and return beans to saucepan with enough cold water to cover; bring to a boil. Reduce heat and simmer, uncovered, 1 hour or until beans are tender but not mushy. Drain; reserving liquid.

2 In large skillet, heat olive oil over medium-high heat until hot. Add onion and cook 5 minutes or until softened. Stir in beans and ½ cup liquid; reduce heat to medium and cook uncovered 5 to 8 minutes. Stir in cranberries, walnuts, garlic and more liquid if necessary. Cook an additional 5 minutes. Stir in cilantro and coriander. Season with salt and pepper. Serve warm or cold.

6 servings.

GREEN CHILE CHEESE GRITS

Deanna Smith, Canton, GA

4 cups water

1 cup grits

Dash salt

1 cup shredded sharp cheddar cheese

1 cup shredded Pepper Jack cheese

8 tablespoons butter

1 (4-oz.) can chopped green chiles

3 eggs, beaten

Salt, to taste

Freshly ground pepper, to taste

Cayenne pepper, if desired

1 Heat oven to 350°F. Spray 2- to 3-quart baking dish with cooking spray.

2 Bring water to a boil in large saucepan. Add grits; cover and cook according to package directions with dash of salt, about 5 minutes. Stir in cheeses and butter; stir until melted. Add chiles, eggs, salt, pepper and cayenne pepper; stir to combine. Pour into prepared baking dish. Bake 45 minutes or until heated through. Serve immediately. Fry leftover patties and serve with eggs, if desired.

8 to 10 servings.

STUFFED CABBAGE BALLS

Carl Boutifier, Freeport, OH

1 large head of cabbage

1 lb. ground beef

1 lb. bulk pork sausage

1 cup plain or seasoned bread crumbs

¼ cup beef broth

½ cup chopped onion

½ cup chopped peppers

1 egg

Pinch salt

¼ teaspoon freshly ground pepper

1 cup cooked rice

Tomato sauce, if desired

1 Cook cabbage in large saucepan until wilted.

2 In large bowl, mix together ground beef, pork sausage, bread crumbs, beef broth, onion, peppers, egg, salt, pepper and rice. Form mixture into egg-size balls; place each in a cabbage leaf and fasten with toothpick.

3 In large skillet, lightly brown cabbage leaves over medium-high heat. Cover and simmer approximately 2 hours or until meat is no longer pink in center, adding a little bit of water if necessary. Serve with tomato sauce, if desired.

6 to 8 servings.

CANDIED WALNUT AND GOAT CHEESE SALAD FOR TWO

Tami Berman, Toronto, ON, Canada

½ cup chopped walnuts

½ tablespoon balsamic vinegar

1 tablespoon sugar

4 cups chopped romaine lettuce

½ cup sliced red onion

4 oz. semi-moist goat cheese

¼ cup dried cranberries

Extra-virgin olive oil, to taste

Raspberry balsamic vinegar or balsamic vinegar, to taste

❶ Heat small skillet over medium heat. Add walnuts and cook until toasted, about 3 minutes. Add balsamic vinegar and toss to coat. Stir in sugar and remove from heat.

❷ In two salad bowls, add bite-size pieces of lettuce and several pieces of thinly sliced red onion. Break goat cheese into the bowls and add cranberries. Sprinkle walnuts over each salad and splash olive oil and balsamic vinegar; toss lightly. Serve with beef, lamb, or chicken and white wine.

2 servings.

BROCCOLI BACON SALAD

Doug Wendling, Corolla, NC

SALAD

2½ cups fresh broccoli florets, cut into small pieces

5 to 6 bacon strips, cooked and crumbled

½ cup golden raisins

½ cup raisins

½ cup diced red onion

½ to ¾ cup chopped almonds or pecans

DRESSING

1 cup mayonnaise

½ cup sugar

2 tablespoons vinegar

❶ For Salad: Mix broccoli, bacon strips, raisins, red onion and chopped almonds in large bowl.

❷ For Dressing: Blend mayonnaise and sugar in small bowl. Slowly whisk in vinegar. Drizzle dressing over broccoli mixture and serve.

4 to 6 servings.

FRUIT SALAD

Paula Weinheimer, Hodgkins, IL

1 to 2 bananas

3 to 4 apples

1 to 2 pears

1 to 2 oranges

1 (12- to 16-oz.) can mixed fruit, drained

½ to 2 cups mayonnaise or salad dressing

Raisins, if desired

Chopped nuts, if desired

❶ Slice or cube fresh fruit. Stir in drained mixed fruit and add mayonnaise to taste. If desired, sprinkle with raisins and nuts.

4 to 6 servings.

Broccoli Bacon Salad

CAPRIZZI DI RADIATORE

Brian Bilderback, Springfield, OR

2 cups radiatore pasta

1 bunch fresh basil leaves

6 oz. fresh mozzarella, cut into ½-inch cubes

4 Roma tomatoes, seeded, cut into ½-inch cubes

½ cup extra-virgin olive oil

¼ cup red wine vinegar

2 garlic cloves, minced

Salt, to taste

Freshly ground pepper, to taste

1 Cook pasta according to package directions; drain and cool.

2 Meanwhile julienne the basil. Combine pasta, cheese, tomato and basil in large glass bowl. In small bowl, combine olive oil, vinegar, garlic and salt and pepper; mix well and drizzle over pasta. Cover and refrigerate 1 hour before serving.

4 to 6 servings.

BLUE CHEESE COLESLAW

Alice Grove, Bethel, OH

½ cup blue cheese

½ cup buttermilk

2 to 3 tablespoons cider vinegar

2 tablespoons sugar

Salt, to taste

Freshly ground pepper, to taste

1 head cabbage, shredded, about 8 to 12 cups

1 Blend blue cheese, buttermilk, cider vinegar, sugar, salt and pepper in medium bowl until smooth.

2 Place cabbage in large bowl; pour on dressing to taste. Chill 1 hour before serving.

16 to 24 servings.

CORN BREAD SALAD

Michelle Walker, Brandon, FL

2 boxes Jiffy corn bread mix

½ cup diced jalapeño pepper

¼ teaspoon ground cumin

¼ teaspoon dried sage

24 oz. sour cream

24 oz. mayonnaise

2 (15.5-oz.) cans pinto beans

2 cups chopped onion

1 (1-oz.) pkg. ranch dressing mix

2 to 3 tomatoes, chopped

1 green pepper, chopped

1 onion, chopped

1 (15-oz.) can corn, drained

Shredded cheese

2 cups diced olives

1 cup whole black olives, pitted

1 Mix corn bread according to package directions and stir in jalapeño, cumin and sage. Bake according to package directions; cool and crumble into bite-size pieces.

2 Mix sour cream, mayonnaise, pinto beans, 1 cup of the onion and dressing in large bowl; set aside.

3 Mix tomatoes, pepper, remaining onion and corn in another large bowl; set aside.

4 In small bowl, stir together cheese and olives.

5 Layer bottom of 13x9-inch pan with crumbled corn bread. Top with sour cream, mayonnaise mixture and then tomato mixture. Sprinkle with cheese mixture.

12 to 16 servings.

ORANGE CREAM DELIGHT FRUIT SALAD

Crystal Harris, Corpus Christi, TX

1 (3½-oz.) pkg. instant vanilla pudding mix

1½ cups milk

⅓ cup frozen orange juice concentrate, thawed

¾ cup sour cream

1 (20-oz.) can pineapple bits, drained

1 (15-oz.) can sliced peaches, drained

1 (11-oz.) can mandarin orange segments, drained

2 bananas, sliced

1 apple, peeled, cored, and sliced

1 In medium mixing bowl, combine pudding, milk and orange juice concentrate. Mix with electric mixer on medium speed 2 minutes. Stir in sour cream; set aside.

2 In large bowl, combine pineapple, peaches, oranges, bananas and apple; stir in pudding mixture. Cover and refrigerate 2 hours before serving.

8 to 12 servings.

RED PEPPERS AND GREEN BEANS

Emily Blakesley, Grass Valley, CA

3 tablespoons extra-virgin olive oil

1 lb. fresh green beans

1 medium red bell pepper, cut into bite-size pieces

¼ cup finely chopped red onion

Salt, to taste

Freshly ground pepper, to taste

¼ cup red wine

1 In large skillet, heat oil over high heat until hot. Add green beans, red bell pepper, onion, salt and pepper; cook 5 minutes. Add red wine; reduce heat to medium and continue cooking an additional 5 to 6 minutes or until liquid has evaporated.

8 to 12 servings.

MEDITERRANEAN PASTA SALAD

Peggy M. Yamaguchi-Lazar, Eugene, OR

1 to 1½ lbs. pasta

2 (4-oz.) jars diced pimiento

1 (6-oz.) can sliced black olives, if desired

1 (12-oz.) jar marinated artichoke hearts

1 (15½-oz.) can garbanzo beans

1 cucumber, quartered

3 to 4 Roma tomatoes, chopped

⅓ lb. baby carrots, sliced

8 to 10 oz. feta cheese, crumbled

½ cup olive oil

¼ to ⅓ cup red wine vinegar or ¾ to 1 cup Italian dressing

1 tablespoon dried oregano

1 tablespoon granulated garlic

1 to 1½ teaspoons Spike seasoning

1 teaspoon Italian seasoning

1 Cook pasta according to package directions.

2 Mix together pimientos, olives, artichoke hearts, garbanzo beans, cucumber, tomatoes, carrots, feta cheese, olive oil, red wine vinegar, oregano, garlic, Spike seasoning and Italian seasoning in large bowl. Refrigerate several hours or overnight.

16 servings.

PINEAPPLE SALAD

Virginia Lehtola, Elk River, MN

1 (20-oz.) can crushed pineapple, in juice

Water

2 tablespoons all-purpose flour

4 tablespoons sugar

2 pasteurized eggs, lightly beaten (or egg beaters)

1 cup heavy cream, whipped

Sugar, to taste

Red grapes, to taste

Bananas or assorted fruit, to taste

Chopped nuts, to taste

1 Drain juice from pineapple; add enough water to make 1 cup. Mix flour and sugar with the juice in medium skillet. Add eggs to skillet and cook on medium-low heat, stirring constantly until bubbly and lightly thickened. Stir in pineapple; pour into large bowl. Cover and refrigerate.

2 To serve, sweeten the whipped cream with sugar to taste; fold into pineapple mixture along with grapes, bananas or desired fruit and chopped nuts, if desired.

8 to 10 servings.

POTATO SALAD

Jane Zimmerman, Chicago, IL

8 to 10 large red potatoes, unpeeled

4 hard-boiled eggs, peeled and chopped

1½ cups salad dressing

½ cup chopped celery

2 tablespoons finely chopped onion

1 tablespoon chopped pimiento

1 tablespoon prepared mustard

1 tablespoon sweet pickle relish

Salt, to taste

Freshly ground pepper, to taste

1 Cook potatoes in large saucepan of boiling water until tender; drain, cool, cut into cubes and place in large bowl. Gently stir in eggs.

2 In small bowl, combine salad dressing, celery, onion, pimiento, mustard, relish, salt and pepper. Stir salad dressing mixture into potato mixture to combine.

8 to 10 servings.

PARTY JELLO SALAD

Devona Greene, Shoreline, WA

1 (8-serving size) pkg. lemon or apricot Jello

2 cups boiling water

6 tablespoons vinegar

½ cup chopped nuts

½ cup chopped sweet pickles

½ cup chopped pimientos

½ cup sliced black olives

½ cup freshly grated Parmesan cheese

1 cup heavy cream, whipped

1 In large bowl, mix Jello, boiling water and vinegar. Place bowl in refrigerator until partially thickened; whisk mixture and fold in nuts, sweet pickles, pimientos, black olives, cheese and cream. Spoon into 9x9-inch dish or mold; refrigerate until firm.

8 to 12 servings.

SPINACH SALAD WITH FIGS AND FETA

Brenda Haley, Thorsby, AB, Canada

8 oz. dried light figs, quartered

¾ cup port wine

Juice of 1 lemon

⅓ cup olive oil

1 garlic clove, minced

4 teaspoons honey

¼ teaspoon salt

¼ teaspoon freshly ground pepper

12 oz. baby spinach

½ cup crumbled feta cheese

¼ cup slivered almonds, toasted

1 Boil figs with port in small saucepan. Cover, simmer 5 minutes. Remove figs and boil port until reduced to 2 tablespoons.

2 In large bowl, whisk together lemon juice, oil, garlic, honey, salt, pepper and reserved port syrup. Toss with spinach.

3 Divide salad among 8 plates. Top with feta, almonds and reserved figs.

8 servings.

VEGGIE SALAD

Josephine Minicuci, Palm Bay, FL

1 cup sugar

½ cup apple cider vinegar

¼ cup vegetable oil

1 (15-oz.) can cut green beans, drained

1 (15-oz.) can white corn, drained

1 (15-oz.) can peas, drained

1 small onion, finely diced

1 rib celery, finely diced

½ cup finely diced carrots

½ cup finely diced red and green bell pepper

1 In large bowl, whisk together sugar, vinegar and oil. Stir in green beans, white corn, peas, onion, celery, carrots and bell pepper. Serve cold.

12 servings.

GINGER AND GARLIC MASHED SWEET POTATOES

Debby Page, Andover, CT

3 (12- to 16-oz. each) large sweet potatoes or yams, washed, unpeeled

1 teaspoon grated fresh ginger

2 garlic cloves, pressed

½ teaspoon hot pepper sauce

3 tablespoons butter

¼ to ½ cup milk

2 to 3 green onions, thinly sliced

1 Place potatoes in large saucepan and cover with cold water. Bring to a boil. Boil 20 to 30 minutes or until fork-tender; drain, cool and peel off skins. Place potatoes back into saucepan; add ginger, garlic cloves, hot pepper sauce, butter and milk, adding enough milk to achieve desired consistency. Mash and sprinkle with green onions.

6 servings.

Honey Mustard Spinach Salad

HONEY MUSTARD SPINACH SALAD

Celeste Ching, Honolulu, HI

DRESSING

1¾ cups mayonnaise

¼ cup apple cider vinegar

¼ cup prepared mustard

½ cup honey

Worcestershire sauce, to taste

1 cup vegetable oil

Salt, to taste

White pepper, to taste

SALAD

16 oz. spinach leaves

3 hard-boiled eggs, chopped

1 red onion, thinly sliced

3 Roma tomatoes, cut into wedges

1 (8-oz.) pkg. button mushrooms

Bacon bits, to taste

Croutons, to taste

1 Mix mayonnaise, vinegar, mustard, honey and Worcestershire in medium bowl until smooth. Gradually whisk in salad oil. Season with salt and pepper. Cover and refrigerate at least 8 hours.

2 Ladle salad dressing onto sides and bottom of large mixing bowl. Add spinach and toss gently until coated with dressing. Add additional dressing as needed to coat leaves.

3 Sprinkle eggs, onions, tomatoes, mushrooms and bacon bits over spinach. Top with croutons. Refrigerate leftover dressing.

6 to 8 servings.

BOURBON STREET SWEET POTATOES WITH BUTTERED PECANS

Elaine Sweet, Dallas, TX

4 quarts water

1 tablespoon kosher (coarse) salt

6 sweet potatoes, peeled and cubed

2 tablespoons unsalted butter, softened

½ cup half-and-half

⅓ cup bourbon

⅓ cup low-sugar raspberry preserves

⅓ cup low-sugar apricot preserves

2 tablespoons packed light brown sugar

½ teaspoon ground cinnamon

½ teaspoon ground nutmeg

¼ teaspoon ground allspice

1½ teaspoons salt

1 tablespoon unsalted butter

½ cup chopped pecans

1 In large saucepan, bring water and salt to a boil. Add sweet potato; cook until fork-tender, then drain. Add butter and half-and-half to saucepan and mash sweet potatoes. Stir in bourbon, fruit preserves, brown sugar, cinnamon, nutmeg, allspice and salt. Keep warm.

2 Heat medium skillet over medium heat. Add butter; sauté pecans until golden, about 4 minutes. Transfer mashed sweet potatoes to serving dish; sprinkle with toasted pecans.

6 servings.

CAULIFLOWER BLOSSOM

Alice Grove, Bethel, OH

¼ cup seasoned bread crumbs

¼ cup freshly grated Parmesan cheese

1 teaspoon dried dill

¼ teaspoon salt

⅛ teaspoon freshly ground pepper

1 medium head cauliflower, trimmed

4 tablespoons butter, melted

1 Heat oven to 350°F. Spray 8-inch square baking dish with cooking spray.

2 In small bowl, combine bread crumbs, Parmesan cheese, dill, salt and pepper; set aside.

3 Bring ½ inch water to a boil in large saucepan. Place cauliflower, stem-side down, in saucepan. Cover and steam over medium heat 12 to 15 minutes or until tender. Remove to prepared baking dish.

4 Pour melted butter evenly over the top and sprinkle with bread crumb mixture, pressing it onto the cauliflower. Spray cauliflower with cooking spray. Bake 30 to 40 minutes or until crumbs are lightly browned and cauliflower is fork-tender. Serve with additional melted butter for dipping, if desired.

6 to 8 servings.

BROCCOLI AND CAULIFLOWER CASSEROLE

Jayne Leight, Stacy, MN

6 large potatoes, unpeeled, sliced ¼ inch thick

1 (10¾-oz.) can cream of chicken or cream of mushroom soup

1 (16-oz.) pkg. frozen broccoli and cauliflower

Half can of water

½ lb. ground beef, browned

2 cups shredded cheddar cheese

1 Heat oven to 350°F.

2 Cook potatoes in large saucepan of boiling water 10 minutes. Layer potatoes in 2- to 3-quart baking dish.

3 Spread one-fourth can of soup over potatoes. Layer broccoli and cauliflower over potatoes. Spread remaining soup and water over vegetables. Sprinkle browned hamburger over vegetables. Bake 1 hour. Sprinkle with cheese and continue baking until cheese is melted.

6 to 8 servings.

CHEEZY BAGUETTE

Joy Smrcina, Cleveland, OH

1 (1-lb.) French baguette loaf

Butter-flavored cooking spray

1 (4-oz.) container aged sharp provolone spreadable cheese

1 (8-oz.) stick pepperoni (about 1-inch diameter), thinly sliced

Pasta sauce

1 Heat oven to broil.

2 Cut bread into 1-inch-thick slices. Place on baking sheet; spray with butter spray. Spread a generous helping of the provolone spread on each slice; top with pepperoni. Broil until cheese melts and is beginning to brown. Serve with warm pasta sauce for dipping.

16 to 24 servings.

CHEESY HASH BROWNS WITH SOUR CREAM

L. Tims, Phoenix, AZ

4 tablespoons butter

2½ cups shredded cheddar cheese

1 (1-lb.) pkg. refrigerated hash browns

½ cup minced onion or green onion

1 cup sour cream

Salt, to taste

Freshly ground pepper, to taste

Paprika, to taste

1 Heat oven to 350°F. Spray 9x9-inch baking dish with cooking spray.

2 Melt butter and 2 cups of cheese in small heavy saucepan over medium heat, stirring constantly; remove from heat.

3 In large bowl, combine potatoes, onions, sour cream, cheese mixture, salt and pepper. Pour into prepared dish. Sprinkle with remaining cheese and paprika. Bake 30 minutes or until bubbly.

8 to 10 servings.

LEEKS FOR TWO

Donna Brooks, Crofton, BC, Canada

4 large leeks

1 (8-oz.) container feta cheese

4 strips bacon, cooked and crumbled

1 (1-lb.) loaf baguette bread, cut into slices

Garlic slices

1 Cut leeks in half then into 1-inch pieces. Heat large skillet over medium-high heat; add leeks and cook until browned. Remove from skillet and crumble feta and bacon over leeks.

2 Toast baguette and spread sliced garlic over toasted slices; top with leek mixture.

6 to 8 servings.

BEANS CREOLE STYLE

Barbara Hamilton, Pompton Lakes, NJ

½ lb. bacon, cooked, crumbled

1 onion, chopped

1 green bell pepper, chopped

1 tablespoon all-purpose flour

2 teaspoons seasoned salt

¼ teaspoon freshly ground pepper

2 tablespoons packed brown sugar

2 teaspoons prepared mustard

1 teaspoon Worcestershire sauce

1 (19-oz.) can whole tomatoes

1 (40-oz.) can butter beans

1 Cook bacon in large skillet over medium heat until crisp; remove to paper towels. Add onion and pepper to bacon drippings in skillet and cook 5 minutes.

2 In small bowl, stir together flour, seasoned salt, pepper, brown sugar, mustard and Worcestershire sauce; stir into onion mixture to combine. Add tomatoes and simmer, uncovered, 10 minutes. Add butter beans and heat thoroughly. Sprinkle each serving with bacon.

8 to 10 servings.

CHEROKEE SWEET POTATO PATTIES

Brenda Beyer, Port Richey, FL

3/4 cup mashed sweet potato

2/3 cup milk

4 tablespoons butter, melted

1 cup all-purpose flour

4 teaspoons baking powder

1 1/4 tablespoons sugar

Dash salt

1 Heat oven to 375°F. Spray baking sheet with cooking spray.

2 Mix potato, milk, and butter together in large bowl. Add flour, baking powder, sugar and salt; combine to form a soft dough. Form mixture into patties and place on prepared baking sheet. Bake 15 minutes or until heated through. Serve with butter.

6 to 8 servings.

CORN CASSEROLE

Angelana Cristan, Marquette, MI

1 (15-oz.) can whole kernel sweet corn

1/2 cup milk

1 cup cracker crumbs

1/2 small onion, chopped

Salt, to taste

Freshly ground pepper, to taste

2 tablespoons butter

1 Heat oven to 350°F. Spray 2-quart baking dish with cooking spray.

2 In large bowl, mix together corn, milk, cracker crumbs, onion, salt, pepper and butter. Spoon into prepared baking dish and bake 30 minutes or until heated through.

6 servings.

CRAN-APPLE SAUCE

Sandra T. Pugh, Crawfordville, GA

4 large Granny Smith apples, peeled, sliced

Water

1/4 to 1/3 cup sugar

1 cup water

1 cup sugar

1 (16-oz.) pkg. fresh cranberries

1 Place apples in heavy, large saucepan and cover with water. Cook over medium heat, stirring occasionally, until sauce is almost smooth. Add sugar to taste. Set aside.

2 In small, heavy saucepan, boil water and sugar until sugar is dissolved. Add cranberries; bring back to a boil. Cook until cranberries have burst, about 10 minutes. If desired, put cranberries through a strainer to remove skins. Combine applesauce and cranberry sauce in large bowl. Refrigerate until serving. Serve with turkey, ham, chicken or pork.

12 to 16 servings.

CHUNKY APPLE-PEAR SAUCE

Janet Utz, Kenmore, NY

5 to 6 apples, peeled and cored

2 to 3 large ripe pears, peeled and cored

1 to 2 teaspoons honey

Ground cinnamon, to taste

Chopped nuts, if desired

1 Cut fruit into small pieces; place in a large saucepan and cover. Simmer, stirring occasionally, until fruit has cooked down. Stir in honey and cinnamon. Sprinkle with chopped nuts, if desired. Serve warm or cold.

8 servings.

DILLY ROLLS

Rebecca Rubes, Wynnewood, OK

¼ cup water

1 cup cottage cheese

1 pkg. yeast

1 tablespoon sugar

1 tablespoon butter

½ teaspoon garlic salt

1 tablespoon minced onion

2 teaspoons dried dill

¼ teaspoon baking soda

1 egg

2¼ to 2½ cups all-purpose flour

Melted butter

1 Heat water and cottage cheese in medium saucepan until lukewarm. Pour into large mixing bowl and stir in yeast. Add sugar, butter, garlic salt, onion, dill, baking soda and egg; stir to combine. Add flour, 1 cup at a time, until a nice dough is formed. Let rise in warm place until double in size, about 60 minutes. Punch down and pinch off dough to make rolls. Place on baking sheet and let rise until doubled in size.

2 Heat oven to 350°F and bake 15 to 20 minutes or until golden brown. Brush with butter.

Servings vary.

FROSTED BROCCOLI BAKE

Jill Wright, Dixon, IL

1 large or 2 small bunches broccoli

Chicken broth

4 tablespoons mayonnaise

4 tablespoons sour cream

2 tablespoons cream cheese

2 cloves roasted garlic, mashed

1 teaspoon dried minced onion

½ teaspoon dried dill

½ teaspoon dried parsley

Dash hot sauce

Freshly ground pepper, to taste

¼ cup dry or Panko bread crumbs

2 teaspoons freshly grated Parmesan cheese

Paprika, if desired

1 Heat oven to 350°F.

2 Cut off broccoli stem, leaving about ½ inch intact; steam 5 minutes until crisp-tender. Place broccoli upright in deep baking dish. Pour ½-inch layer of chicken broth into bottom of dish.

3 Combine mayonnaise, sour cream, cream cheese, garlic, onion, dill, parsley, hot sauce and black pepper in large bowl. Spread over top of broccoli. Sprinkle bread crumbs, Parmesan and paprika over top of broccoli. Bake 20 to 25 minutes until topping is a light golden brown and broccoli is tender.

4 to 6 servings.

GRANNY'S AU GRATIN POTATOES

Hope Wasylenki, Gahanna, OH

1 pint half-and-half or milk

2 sticks butter

¾ lb. processed cheese loaf, cubed

1 cup shredded cheddar cheese

1 (48-oz.) pkg. frozen hash browns, thawed

1 sweet onion, finely diced

1 cup diced bell pepper

Paprika, if desired

1 Heat oven to 350°F.

2 In large saucepan, combine half-and-half, butter and cheeses. Stir constantly over medium heat until smooth; remove from heat.

3 In 13x9-inch pan mix potatoes, onion and bell pepper. Pour cheese sauce over potatoes. Lightly sprinkle with paprika, if desired. Bake 60 to 90 minutes or until potatoes are fork-tender and sauce is bubbling. Let stand 20 minutes before serving.

8 to 10 servings.

SWEET POTATOES WITH BRANDIED MARMALADE GLAZE

Lily Mathews Naidu, Federal Way, WA

2 lbs. sweet potatoes, peeled and sliced into ½-inch slices

¾ cup orange juice concentrate

¾ cup bitter orange marmalade

3 teaspoons grated fresh ginger

2 teaspoons prepared mustard

3 tablespoons butter, divided

2 tablespoons brandy

1 Heat oven to 350°F.

2 Steam potatoes 10 minutes or until fork-tender.

3 Mix orange juice, marmalade, ginger, mustard, and 1 tablespoon butter in medium saucepan and simmer 10 minutes. Remove from heat and stir in remaining butter and brandy. Place potatoes in shallow baking dish and pour glaze over each piece. Bake 30 minutes.

6 to 8 servings.

BROCCOLI CASSEROLE

Mable Watson, Lenoir, NC

1 large head broccoli, chopped, cooked and drained

1 cup shredded sharp cheddar cheese

2 eggs, beaten

2 teaspoons onion flakes

1 Heat oven to 350°F.

2 Place cooked broccoli in 2- to 3-quart baking dish.

3 In medium bowl, mix cheese, eggs and onion flakes. Pour over broccoli. Bake 20 minutes until set.

6 to 8 servings.

Sweet Potatoes with Brandied Marmalade Glaze

HASH BROWN CASSEROLE

Gail Dupree, Lillington, NC

½ cup butter, melted

1 (2-lb.) pkg. frozen hash browns, thawed

½ cup chopped onion

1 pint sour cream

1 (10¾-oz.) can cream of chicken soup

¾ teaspoon salt

½ teaspoon freshly ground pepper

2 cups (1 lb.) processed cheese loaf, melted

1 cup crushed potato chips

1 Heat oven to 350°F.

2 In large bowl, pour butter over hash browns.

3 In medium bowl, mix together onion, sour cream, chicken soup, salt, pepper and cheese loaf. Toss onion mixture with hash browns until hash browns are coated.

4 Spread mixture into prepared baking dish. Top with crushed potato chips. Bake 1 hour or until potatoes are tender.

8 to 10 servings.

STUFFED POTATOES

Terri Thibault, Calgary, AB, Canada

10 russet potatoes, baked

2 oz. cream cheese, softened

4 green onions, sliced

6 to 10 strips of bacon, cooked and crumbled

¼ to ½ cup sour cream

1 cup shredded cheddar cheese

2 tablespoons butter

1 Heat oven to 350°F.

2 Cut potatoes in half and scoop out insides; place in large bowl and add cream cheese, onions, bacon, sour cream, cheddar cheese and butter; mash together and re-stuff potatoes. Bake 15 minutes or grill 5 minutes until golden brown.

10 servings.

MOIST ALWAYS CORN BREAD

Connie Vesey, Squaw Lake, MN

1 cup all-purpose flour

1 cup yellow cornmeal

½ cup sugar

4 teaspoons baking powder

1 teaspoon salt

2 cups milk

½ cup applesauce

2 eggs

1 Heat oven to 400°F. Spray 9-inch baking pan with cooking spray.

2 In medium bowl stir together flour, cornmeal, sugar, baking powder and salt.

3 In separate medium bowl stir together milk, applesauce and eggs. Stir dry ingredients into wet ingredients until combined. Pour into prepared pan and bake 30 minutes.

8 to 10 servings.

MOM'S SQUASH CASSEROLE

JoAnne Taylor, Bensenville, IL

SQUASH

6 cups cooked squash

½ cup melted butter

6 eggs, beaten

1 cup packed brown sugar

½ teaspoon salt

TOPPING

½ cup packed brown sugar

½ cup melted butter

1½ cups crispy rice cereal

1 Heat oven to 350°F.

2 In large bowl, stir together squash, butter, eggs, brown sugar and salt until combined. Pour mixture into baking dish and bake 50 minutes or until set.

3 In medium bowl, stir together brown sugar, butter and rice cereal until smooth. Pour into ungreased 13x9-inch baking dish. Bake until set and pour over squash.

8 to 10 servings.

MUSHROOM AND SAUSAGE STUFFING

Kathy Allred, Tucson, AZ

1 lb. breakfast sausage (such as Jimmy Dean maple flavor)

8 oz. mushrooms, sliced

4 cups unseasoned dry bread cubes

4 tablespoons butter, melted

2 eggs, beaten

2 tablespoons dried parsley

¼ teaspoon salt

Freshly ground pepper, to taste

⅛ teaspoon dried basil

⅛ teaspoon dried marjoram

3 teaspoons dried sage

1 large fresh apple, peeled and cut into small pieces (or ½ cup applesauce)

1 to 1½ cups chicken broth

1 Cook sausage and mushrooms in large skillet until sausage is cooked through and mushrooms are browned; drain.

2 In large bowl, place bread cubes, butter, eggs, parsley, salt, pepper, basil, marjoram, sage and apple; toss gently to mix. Add broth, a little at a time, until mixture is very moist. Add sausage, mushroom mixture and stir to combine; add more broth, if necessary.

3 Heat oven to 350°F. Spray 11x7-inch baking dish with cooking spray. Spread stuffing into baking dish and cover loosely with aluminum foil. Bake 35 to 45 minutes.

12 servings.

FRIED BISCUITS

Barbara Boyer, Saint Robert, MO

2 cups all-purpose flour

½ teaspoon salt

2½ teaspoons baking powder

2 tablespoons shortening

⅔ to ¾ cup milk

Oil

Syrup or honey

1 Sift flour, salt and baking powder together in large bowl. Cut in shortening with a fork. Add enough milk to make a biscuit-like dough. Roll dough onto a floured surface and cut into 1-inch-wide strips. Cut each strip into 3-inch lengths. Deep fry in hot oil until golden brown on both sides. Serve with syrup or honey.

Servings vary.

SPICY GREEN BEANS

Brian Redman, Louisville, KY

4 slices smoked bacon, diced

1 onion, diced

2 lbs. fresh green beans, trimmed

1 cup boiling water

Salt to taste

2 tablespoons butter, softened

3 tablespoons white vinegar

Juice of ½ lemon

Freshly ground pepper, to taste

1 tablespoon cayenne pepper, or to taste

1 Cook bacon in large skillet until almost crisp. Remove and drain on paper towels. Add onion to bacon grease and cook until softened. Add green beans, water and salt. Bring to a boil. Cover; reduce heat and simmer 30 minutes or until beans are crisp-tender. Stir in butter, vinegar, lemon and peppers. Stir beans to coat well. Serve immediately.

4 to 6 servings.

ZUCCHINI CASSEROLE

Tina Wood, Jenera, OH

6 cups green and yellow zucchini, sliced

¼ cup onion

1 cup shredded carrots

Salt, to taste

Freshly ground pepper, to taste

1 (10¾-oz.) can condensed cream of mushroom soup

1 cup sour cream

¼ bag stuffing (such as Pepperidge Farm), crushed

6 tablespoon butter, melted

1 Heat oven to 350°F.

2 Boil zucchini, onion and carrots in large saucepan 5 minutes; drain. Pour into large bowl and sprinkle with salt and pepper. Stir in soup and sour cream until combined.

3 In large bowl, toss together stuffing and butter. Place half of stuffing mixture on bottom of 2- to 3-quart baking dish. Cover with vegetable mixture. Sprinkle remaining stuffing mixture over vegetable mixture. Bake 30 minutes.

8 to 10 servings.

Soups
AND
Sandwiches

CHICKEN SPREAD

Johanne Chabot, Quebec, Canada

1 (16-oz.) can seasoned chicken breast meat, drained

3 green onions, sliced

Salt, to taste

Freshly ground pepper, to taste

½ cup mayonnaise

1 Place chicken and green onions in food processor; process 2 minutes or until almost smooth. Spoon into large bowl; stir in salt, pepper and mayonnaise to combine. Refrigerate 1 hour. Spread on bread, pita, toast or whole wheat crackers.

10 to 12 servings.

POTATO AND EGG SANDWICHES

Stacia Chivilo, Indian Head Park, IL

8 to 9 eggs, beaten

Salt, to taste

Freshly ground pepper, to taste

Dried parsley, to taste

Onion powder, to taste

Garlic powder, to taste

Olive oil, to taste

3 to 4 potatoes, peeled, chopped

French rolls, hollowed or loaf of Italian bread, halved and hollowed

1 In medium bowl, stir together eggs, salt, pepper, parsley, onion powder and garlic powder.

2 In large skillet heat oil over medium-high heat until hot. Add potatoes; cook until fork-tender and browned. Pour in eggs and continue cooking, stirring frequently until cooked through. Serve inside hollowed rolls or bread. If using bread, cut into 4 pieces.

4 to 6 servings.

GRILLED SPICY SOUTHWESTERN PHILLY

Shellie Shaull, Overland Park, KS

1 teaspoon olive oil

1 teaspoon minced garlic

½ tablespoon Worcestershire sauce

4 oz. breakfast steak, cut into bite-size pieces

1 teaspoon Greek seasoning

1 tablespoon diced tomato

1 tablespoon diced red onion

1 teaspoon chopped jalapeño

2 slices bacon, cooked and crumbled

¼ cup shredded cheddar cheese

¼ cup shredded Pepper Jack cheese

1 (10- to 12-inch) flour tortilla

1 tablespoon butter, softened

Salsa, if desired

Sour cream, if desired

1 In large skillet, heat oil over medium heat until hot. Add garlic and cook until slightly browned. Add Worcestershire sauce, steak and Greek seasoning; cook until steak is browned. Remove from heat.

2 In medium bowl, combine steak, tomato, red onion, jalapeño, bacon and cheeses; stir until combined. Spread one side of tortilla with butter and place buttered-side down on work surface. Spoon steak mixture down center of tortilla. Fold bottom third and then the sides of the tortilla up over the filling. Roll up tortilla to completely enclose filling.

3 Heat medium skillet over medium heat. Place sandwich in skillet, seam-side down; cook until browned on all sides. Serve with salsa and sour cream, if desired.

1 serving.

Grilled Spicy Southwestern Philly

HONEY JOES

Barbara Boyer, Saint Robert, MO

2 tablespoons vegetable oil

¼ cup chopped onion

¼ cup chopped celery

¼ cup grated carrot

1 lb. ground beef

½ cup tomato paste

¼ cup honey

3 tablespoons water

1 tablespoon vinegar

2 teaspoons Worcestershire sauce

1½ teaspoons chili powder

Salt, to taste

Freshly ground pepper to taste

4 hamburger buns

1 In large skillet, heat oil over medium heat until hot. Add onions, celery and carrots; cook until softened. Stir in beef and cook until browned and crumbly. Stir in tomato paste, honey, water, vinegar, Worcestershire sauce, chili powder, salt and pepper; simmer, covered, 3 to 5 minutes or until heated through. Serve on hamburger buns.

4 servings.

PHYLLO TRIANGLES WITH TUNA AND CHEESE

Dzhangirova Sveteana, Seattle, WA

2 (6-oz.) cans tuna, drained and flaked

4 to 5 tablespoons mayonnaise

4 oz. shredded smoked Gouda cheese

3 tablespoons finely chopped green onions

Salt, to taste

Freshly ground pepper, to taste

9 phyllo sheets

½ cup butter, melted

1 egg, beaten

1 Heat oven to 375°F. Line baking sheet with parchment paper.

2 In medium bowl, stir together tuna, mayonnaise, cheese, onions, salt and pepper. Place 1 phyllo sheet on work surface and brush with melted butter. Continue layering with 2 more sheets, brushing each sheet with butter. Cut crosswise into 6 strips.

3 Place 1 tablespoon tuna mixture at the bottom of each strip. Fold like a flag the length of the strip to form a triangle. Place on baking sheet. Repeat with remaining phyllo sheets. Brush top of appetizers with beaten egg and bake 15 minutes or until golden brown and crisp. Cool 5 minutes.

18 appetizers.

PJ EGGS

Pat Westcortt, San Rafael, CA

    ½ jar Kraft Cheez Whiz

    Worcestershire sauce, if desired

    Dried parsley, if desired

    4 English muffins, split, toasted

    Butter

    1 (12-oz.) can deviled ham

    Tomato slices, if desired

    Avocado slices, if desired

    4 eggs, poached

1 Stir together cheese sauce, Worcestershire and parsley in medium bowl. Spread cut sides of muffin with butter. Spread ham on bottom half of each muffin; top with tomato and avocado slices, egg, cheese sauce and remaining muffin half.

4 servings.

BEAN AND SMOKED TURKEY MEAT

Brenda T. Brooks, Greenbelt, MD

    2 cups navy beans, rinsed, drained

    3 cups water

    3 to 4 lbs. smoked turkey wings

    1 cup chopped onion

    ¼ cup chopped green pepper

    1 teaspoon white pepper

1 Place beans in large bowl; cover with water and soak overnight. Drain beans and pour into large saucepan. Stir in 3 cups water, smoked turkey wings, onion, green pepper and pepper. Cover and simmer 2 to 2½ hours or until beans and turkey are tender, adding more water, if necessary, during cooking. Serve with biscuits, if desired.

10 to 12 servings.

BACON POTATO CHOWDER

Tina Sevy, Oklahoma City, OK

    1 lb. bacon, diced

    1 large onion, chopped

    1 (32-oz.) bag frozen hash brown potatoes

    1½ cups boiling water

    2 (10¾-oz.) cans cream of chicken soup

    16 oz. sour cream

    2 tablespoons dried dill or chopped fresh dill

    2 pints half-and-half

1 Cook bacon in large skillet over medium heat until crisp; remove with slotted spoon. Add onion to skillet and cook until softened; remove with slotted spoon.

2 Meanwhile, cook potatoes in medium saucepan in boiling water until tender but not falling apart, about 5 to 8 minutes. Add onion, bacon, soup, sour cream and dill. Stir in half-and-half. Heat to simmering, but do not boil. Let simmer 20 to 30 minutes. Serve with corn bread or crackers or sprinkle with cheese, if desired.

10 to 12 servings.

Cioppino

CIOPPINO

Carolyn Olesen, Tecumseh, NE

⅓ cup olive oil

1 large onion, chopped

1 bunch green onions, sliced

1 green pepper, chopped

3 large garlic cloves, minced

⅓ cup chopped fresh parsley

1 (15-oz.) can tomato sauce

1 (28-oz.) can tomatoes

1 cup dry red wine

½ bay leaf

1 tablespoon salt

¼ teaspoon freshly ground pepper

¼ teaspoon dried rosemary

¼ teaspoon dried thyme

10 to 12 fresh clams

8 to 10 fresh mussels

1 lb. shelled, deveined, uncooked medium shrimp

1 lb. scallops

1 lb. crab meat

1 lb. lobster meat, if desired

1 In large saucepan, heat olive oil over medium heat until hot. Add onion, green onions, green pepper, garlic and parsley; cook, stirring frequently, until onion is softened. Add tomato sauce, tomatoes, wine, bay leaf, salt, pepper, rosemary and thyme; cover, reduce heat and simmer 1 hour. Add clams and mussels; cover and simmer until clams and mussels open, about 20 to 30 minutes. Discard any that do not open. Stir in shrimp, scallops, crabmeat and lobster. Simmer until shrimp are cooked through and they turn pink, about 10 minutes. Remove and discard bay leaf. Serve with crusty French or sourdough bread, if desired.

10 to 12 servings.

BAKED POTATO SOUP

Maryellen Scheel, Hazelwood, MO

¼ cup butter

¾ cup chopped onion

¼ cup chopped celery

⅓ cup all-purpose flour

4 cups chicken broth

2 cups half-and-half

8 medium potatoes, baked, peeled and cubed

1 cup cooked crumbled bacon

Salt, to taste

Freshly ground pepper, to taste

1½ cups shredded cheddar cheese

½ cup sliced green onion

1 Heat large saucepan over medium heat. Add butter, onion and celery; cook until softened. Stir in flour until smooth; cook 1 minute. Slowly whisk in chicken broth and half-and-half until smooth. Cook, whisking until smooth and thick, until mixture comes to a boil; reduce heat to low. Add potatoes, bacon, salt, pepper and cheese. Garnish with green onions.

10 to 12 servings.

TOMATO BASIL BISQUE

Kate Wood, Palm Beach Gardens, FL

1 (24-oz.) can diced tomatoes with basil

½ cup 1% milk or fat-free half-and-half

4 oz. reduced-fat or non-fat cream cheese

1 Place tomatoes in blender and pulse until almost smooth. Pour into large saucepan and heat over medium heat until hot but not boiling. Stir in milk; add cream cheese and cook until heated through. Serve with crusty bread, if desired.

6 to 8 servings.

VEGETABLE TORTELLINI

Joseph Werner, Garden City, ID

3 tablespoons canola oil

1 medium yellow onion, diced

2 medium carrots, diced

3 medium ribs celery, diced

½ cup all-purpose flour

2 pints vegetable broth

1 (28-oz.) can diced tomatoes

1 pint half-and-half

1 bay leaf

1 tablespoon dried basil

1 tablespoon dried thyme

1 tablespoon salt

1 tablespoon white pepper

6 oz. frozen cheese tortellini

1 In large saucepan, heat oil over medium heat until hot. Add onion, carrot and celery; cook until vegetables are softened. Stir in flour and cook an additional 1 minute. Whisk in vegetable broth, tomatoes, half-and-half, bay leaf, basil, thyme, salt and pepper; bring to a boil. Add tortellini and continue cooking until pasta is cooked through. Remove and discard bay leaf.

6 to 8 servings.

BORSCH STEW

Jami Kobold, San Diego, CA

2 tablespoons shortening or vegetable oil, divided

1½ to 2 lbs. beef, pork or chicken, cubed

2 lbs. potatoes, peeled, chopped

1 tablespoon salt

1 small bunch beets, peeled, chopped

1 small or ½ large head cabbage, chopped

2 carrots, chopped

½ small onion, finely chopped

4 oz. mushrooms

1 (16- to 24-oz.) can diced tomatoes

1 In large saucepan, melt 1 tablespoon of the shortening over medium-high heat. Add meat; cook until browned. Add 4 to 6 cups hot water, potatoes and salt to saucepan.

2 In large skillet, heat remaining 1 tablespoon shortening over medium-high heat. Add beets, cabbage, carrots and onion; cook until softened. Spoon beet mixture into saucepan. Add mushrooms and tomatoes and boil until mushrooms are tender. Serve hot or cold.

10 to 12 servings.

CHILLED STRAWBERRY SOUP

Linda Murray, Allenstown, NH

1 cup apple juice

1 cup water, divided

⅔ cup sugar

½ teaspoon ground cinnamon

⅛ teaspoon ground cloves

2 cups fresh strawberries

1 (8-oz.) container strawberry yogurt

2 drops red food coloring, if desired

Fresh mint leaves, if desired

1 Stir together apple juice, ¾ cup water, sugar, cinnamon and cloves in medium saucepan. Bring to a boil over medium heat; remove and cool.

2 Place strawberries and remaining water in a blender or food processor; cover and process until smooth. Pour into large bowl. Add apple juice mixture, yogurt and food coloring. Cover; refrigerate until chilled. Garnish with additional strawberries and fresh mint leaves.

6 to 8 servings.

MEAT AND VEGGIE ROLLS

Anne M. Miller, Pipestone, MN

1 (8-oz.) pkg. cream cheese, softened

1 (1-oz.) pkg. dry ranch dressing mix

8 flour tortillas

1 lb. dried beef, finely chopped

1 (6½-oz.) can black olives, finely chopped

1 (4½-oz.) jar pimientos, finely chopped

1 medium green bell pepper, finely chopped

1 Mix cream cheese and dressing together in small bowl and set aside. Spread cream cheese mixture over the tortillas. Sprinkle with beef, olives, pimientos and bell pepper. Roll tortillas and cut into 1-inch pieces. Place on serving platter to serve.

8 servings.

CREAMY CHICKEN NOODLE SOUP

Crystal Harris, Corpus Christi, TX

½ whole chicken, cut up

2 tablespoons butter

2 ribs celery

½ onion, chopped

2 tablespoons all-purpose flour

1 teaspoon salt

¼ teaspoon freshly ground pepper

1½ cups thin egg noodles

½ cup half-and-half

1 Rinse chicken and pat dry.

2 In Dutch oven or large saucepan, cover chicken with water and bring to a boil. Reduce heat and simmer 40 minutes or until chicken is tender and cooked through. Remove chicken, reserving the broth. Shred chicken and remove bones.

3 Heat Dutch oven or large saucepan over medium heat. Add butter, celery and onion; cook until softened. Stir in flour and cook until golden brown. Whisk in reserved broth, salt and pepper. Bring to a boil; stir in noodles and cook until noodles are tender, stirring occasionally. Stir in reserved chicken and half-and-half.

10 to 12 servings.

CREAMY CRAB AND POTATO BISQUE/CHOWDER

Christina L. Mendoza, Alamogordo, NM

3 tablespoons butter

1 large onion, diced

¼ cup instant potato flakes

2 cups frozen corn

4 medium to large potatoes, peeled and cubed

1 (10-oz.) jar Alfredo sauce

2 cups milk

1 cup water

Dried chives, to taste

Salt, to taste

Freshly ground pepper, to taste

2 to 3 dashes garlic powder

1 cup spaetzle, optional

2 (2½-oz.) pkgs. crabmeat

1 Heat large saucepan over medium heat; add butter and onion and cook until onion is softened. Stir in potato flakes and cook until thickened. Stir in corn, potatoes, alfredo sauce, milk, water, chives, salt, pepper and garlic. Simmer on low 45 minutes or until potatoes are crisp-tender. Stir in spaetzle; cover and simmer an additional 15 minutes. Stir in crabmeat. Cover and simmer an additional 15 minutes.

4 to 6 servings.

ROASTED SQUASH AND ITALIAN SAUSAGE SOUP

Ellen Barner, Bridgeville, PA

1 butternut squash, halved, seeds removed

1 acorn squash, halved, seeds removed

Salt, to taste

Freshly ground pepper, to taste

6 tablespoons butter, divided

½ lb. bulk Italian sausage

4 carrots, diced

4 ribs celery, diced

8 garlic cloves, minced

1 fennel bulb, diced (reserve some of the fennel frond for garnish)

1 large onion, diced

¼ cup white wine

6 cups chicken or turkey broth

1 cup heavy cream

1 tablespoon chopped fresh sage

1 teaspoon chopped fresh oregano

Salt, to taste

Freshly ground pepper, to taste

1 Heat oven to 400°F.

2 Place squash skin-side down in large roasting pan; sprinkle with salt and pepper and rub with 1 tablespoon butter. Bake 45 minutes or until soft, adding water to pan if squash begins to brown; remove skins.

3 Heat large skillet over medium heat and cook sausage until browned; drain. Heat separate large saucepan and add remaining butter, carrots, celery, garlic, fennel bulb and onion and cook until soft. Add white wine and cook until reduced by half. Stir in squash, broth and cream to the vegetable mixture; simmer 30 minutes.

4 Puree soup in a food processor or blender, in batches if necessary. Return to saucepan and stir in sausage and remaining ingredients. Garnish bowls with reserved fennel fronds.

10 to 12 servings.

Roasted Squash and Italian Sausage Soup

HALIBUT CHOWDER

Gena Stout, Ravenden, AR

16 oz. cream cheese, softened

1 (11-oz.) can evaporated milk

3 (10¾-oz.) cans cream of potato or mushroom soup

1 (16-oz.) can carrots, drained

1 (15-oz.) can corn, undrained

4 to 5 cups halibut fillet, cut into 1-inch pieces

1 bunch green onions, sliced

2 garlic cloves, minced

Hot pepper sauce, to taste

Chipotle seasoning, to taste

Cajun seasoning, to taste

1 In large saucepan, stir together cream cheese, milk, soup, carrots and corn over medium heat.

2 Heat large skillet over medium heat. Add halibut, onion and garlic; cook until fish is opaque and flakes easily with a fork. Pour fish into saucepan with soup mixture. Season with hot pepper sauce, chipotle or Cajun seasoning.

10 to 12 servings.

LEE'S CARROT-GINGER SOUP

Lee Hofman, San Juan Capistrano, CA

1½ tablespoons olive oil or butter

½ cup peeled and chopped shallots

⅔ cup chopped celery

3 to 4 tablespoons fresh ginger, chopped

2 garlic cloves, minced

2 lbs. carrots, chopped

36 oz. chicken broth

6 tablespoons dry sherry, divided

1 bay leaf

½ teaspoon ground nutmeg

1 to 1½ cups half-and-half

Salt, to taste

White pepper, to taste

Crème Fraîche or sour cream, if desired

1 In large saucepan, heat oil over medium heat. Add shallots and celery; cook until softened. Stir in ginger and garlic and cook an additional 1 minute. Stir in carrots, broth, 3 tablespoons of the sherry and bay leaf. Bring to a boil; cover and simmer on low 1 hour. Remove and discard bay leaf.

2 Pour soup in blender, in batches if necessary, and blend 2 minutes. Strain soup into large bowl. Stir in nutmeg and remaining 3 tablespoons sherry, half-and-half, salt and pepper. Serve warm or chilled. Garnish each bowl with a dollop of Crème Fraîche or sour cream.

10 to 12 servings.

Slow Cooker Meals

CROCK-POT ROASTED PORK

Peggy M. Yamaguchi-Lazar, Eugene, OR

1 (4- to 5-lb.) boneless pork loin roast

½ teaspoon salt

¼ teaspoon freshly ground pepper

1 garlic clove, sliced

2 medium onions, sliced

2 bay leaves

½ cup water

1 tablespoon soy sauce

1 Sprinkle roast with salt and pepper. Make tiny slits in pork roast and insert garlic slices. Place half the onion in bottom of 4- to 5-quart slow cooker; top with roast, remaining onion and bay leaves, water and soy sauce. Cover and cook on low 10 hours or on high 5 to 6 hours until roast is tender.

16 to 20 servings.

THE BEST SLOPPY JOES

JuDee Korta, St. Louis Park, MN

1½ lbs. ground beef

¾ cup finely diced onion

1 (16-oz.) bottle ketchup

1 tablespoon packed brown sugar

2 to 3 teaspoons vinegar

2 to 3 teaspoons chili powder

1 teaspoon lemon juice

Hamburger buns

1 Cook ground beef and onion in large skillet over medium heat until browned. Place beef, onion, ketchup, brown sugar, vinegar, chili powder and lemon juice in 3- to 4-quart slow cooker; cover and cook on low 6 to 8 hours or until heated through. Serve on buns.

6 to 8 servings.

ARTICHOKE SPINACH DIP

Caroline Moody, Lake Butler, FL

1 (10-oz.) pkg. frozen chopped spinach, partially thawed

1 cup mayonnaise

1 cup freshly grated Parmesan or Romano cheese

1 cup artichoke hearts, chopped coarsely

½ chopped red bell pepper

¼ cup sredded Gruyère cheese

1 In medium bowl, mix together spinach, mayonnaise, Parmesan cheese, artichoke hearts, bell pepper and Gruyère cheese. Spoon mixture into 2- to 3-quart slow cooker; cover and cook on low 1 hour and 15 minutes or bake in 9-inch baking dish at 350°F 1 hour.

12 to 16 servings.

BBQ BEEF SANDWICHES

Tina Wood, Jenera, OH

5-lb. boneless beef chuck roast

¼ cup white vinegar

¼ cup packed brown sugar

1 small jar chopped green olives, undrained

1 (7-oz.) can sliced mushrooms, undrained

1 (16-oz.) bottle ketchup

1 tablespoon Worcestershire sauce

1 medium onion, chopped

1 Place roast in 4- to 5-quart slow cooker; cover and cook on low 8 to 10 hours or until fork-tender; shred meat.

2 Add white vinegar, brown sugar, olives, mushrooms, ketchup, Worcestershire sauce, onion and shredded beef to slow cooker and cook an additional 1 hour or until heated through.

16 servings.

Artichoke Spinach Dip

Homemade Chili

HOMEMADE CHILI

Marcy Wilson, Geneva, IL

2 to 3 lbs. ground beef or venison

½ cup chopped onion

1 (28-oz.) can stewed tomatoes, undrained

4 (15-oz.) cans chili beans

1 (15-oz.) can diced tomatoes with onion and garlic, undrained

1 (15-oz.) can dark red kidney beans, drained

1 tomato, chopped

2 garlic cloves, minced

3 tablespoons chili powder

1 tablespoon onion powder

1 tablespoon Italian seasoning

1 tablespoon dried parsley

Dash dried basil

1 Heat large skillet over medium heat and brown ground beef with onion; drain. Place beef, onion, stewed tomatoes, chili beans, diced tomatoes, kidney beans, tomato, garlic cloves, chili powder, onion powder, Italian seasoning, parsley and dried basil in 4- to 5-quart slow cooker; cover and cook on low 8 to 12 hours.

8 to 10 servings.

PEACHY PORK SANDWICHES

Susan Robinson, Johnstown, OH

4- to 5-lb. pork roast, cooked, shredded

2 (14½-oz.) cans peaches, drained or 4 cups fresh peach slices

½ cup applesauce

½ can tomato paste

¼ cup balsamic vinegar

¼ cup soy sauce

1¼ cups packed brown sugar

2 tablespoons minced garlic

¼ teaspoon ground cinnamon

1 Place shredded pork into 4- to 5-quart slow cooker.

2 In blender, combine peaches, applesauce, tomato paste, balsamic vinegar, soy sauce, brown sugar, garlic and cinnamon; process until smooth. Stir into pork in slow cooker. Cover and cook 1 to 2 hours on low or until heated through. Serve on buns.

10 to 12 servings.

POT ROAST

Paula Weinheimer, Naperville, IL

4- lb. beef or pork roast

2 tablespoons Montreal steak seasoning

1 (1-oz.) pkg. onion soup mix

1 tablespoon Worcestershire sauce

2 tablespoons barbecue sauce or ketchup

1 cup salsa or 1 can crushed tomatoes

1 Place roast in 4- to 5-quart slow cooker and add water to cover. Sprinkle with steak seasoning and onion soup mix. Cover and cook on high 4 to 6 hours. Add Worcestershire sauce, barbecue sauce and salsa; cook until meat falls off the bone, about 6 to 8 hours longer. If desired, use juice to make gravy.

4 to 6 servings.

PORK CHOPS WITH APPLE JUICE GRAVY

Laurie Miley, Kalamazoo, MI

4 to 8 boneless pork loin chops, about 1 inch thick

Salt, to taste

Freshly ground pepper, to taste

Onion powder, to taste

Garlic powder, to taste

1 tablespoon vegetable oil

1 medium onion, sliced

1 to 2 garlic cloves, minced

Apple juice, to taste

All-purpose flour, to taste

1 Sprinkle chops with salt, pepper, onion powder and garlic powder.

2 Heat oil in large skillet over medium-high heat; cook pork chops until browned on both sides. Place in 4- to 5-quart slow cooker. Top with onion and garlic. Pour in desired amount of apple juice. Cover and cook on low 7 to 9 hours or on high 4 to 5 hours.

3 Pour juices into medium saucepan and bring to a boil. Mix flour and additional apple juice and whisk into saucepan to thicken. Season with additional salt, pepper, onion and garlic powder, if desired. Serve gravy with pork.

4 to 8 servings.

HOT BUTTERED RUM

Lissa Carrino, Medina, OH

8 cups hot water

2 cups packed brown sugar

8 tablespoons butter

2 teaspoons ground cinnamon

1 teaspoon ground cloves

1 teaspoon ground nutmeg

Dash salt

2 cups dark spiced rum

1 In 4- to 5-quart slow cooker, stir together hot water, brown sugar, butter, cinnamon, cloves, nutmeg and salt; cover and cook on low 5 hours. During last 30 minutes of cooking time, stir in rum. Serve in mugs topped with fresh whipped cream, if desired.

8 to 10 servings.

SPICY QUESO DIP

Laurie Carnevale, Marietta, GA

1 lb. ground beef

2 (16-oz.) pkgs. processed Mexican-flavored cheese loaf, cubed

1 (10-oz.) can diced tomatoes and chili peppers

1 (10-oz.) can diced tomatoes with lime juice and cilantro

Sliced jalapeños, from a jar, to taste

1 Brown ground beef in large skillet over medium heat; Place cheese, beef, tomatoes and jalapeño slices in 4- to 5-quart slow cooker. Stir to combine; cover and cook on high 1 hour, stirring every 20 minutes. Turn slow cooker to low to keep warm. Serve with chips, tortillas or veggies.

24 to 32 servings.

Hot Buttered Rum

HOT ARTICHOKE DIP

Clare Morgan, Duluth, MN

2 (15-oz.) cans artichoke hearts, drained, quartered

16 oz. sour cream

½ cup mayonnaise

1 pkg. leek soup mix

6- to 8-oz. shredded Swiss or Gruyère cheese

⅓ to ½ cup freshly shredded Parmesan cheese

2 tablespoons Italian dressing

Minced garlic, to taste

Dried dill or freshly chopped dill, to taste

1 Heat oven to 375°F.

2 In large bowl, stir together artichoke hearts, sour cream, mayonnaise, soup mix, cheeses, Italian dressing, garlic and dill. Spoon mixture into 13x9-inch baking dish. Bake 30 to 45 minutes or until bubbly and heated through. Transfer to 2- to 3-quart slow cooker to keep warm. Serve with crackers, French bread or bagel chips.

10 to 12 servings.

SPICY WARM TACO DIP

Lissa Carrino, Medina, OH

½ tablespoon oil

¼ cup minced onion

1 (1¼-oz.) pkg. taco seasoning mix

1 (15-oz.) can dark red kidney beans, drained, rinsed

1 (15-oz.) can black beans, drained, rinsed

1 (14-oz.) can diced tomatoes, drained

1 (4-oz.) can chopped green chiles

1½ cups salsa

Tortilla chips

1 In medium saucepan, heat oil over medium heat until hot. Add onion and taco seasoning mix; cook until onions have softened. Stir in kidney beans, black beans, diced tomatoes, green chiles and salsa; cook 5 to10 minutes, mashing beans with spoon. Place in 3- to 4-quart slow cooker to keep warm. Serve with chips.

24 to 32 servings.

BOURBON DOGS

Karyl Kasulis, New Hartford, CT

½ teaspoon dried oregano

½ teaspoon dried rosemary

1 tablespoon dried minced onion

½ cup packed brown sugar

¾ cup bourbon

1½ cups ketchup

1½ to 2 pkgs. Little Smokies wieners

1 In medium saucepan stir together oregano, rosemary, onion, brown sugar, bourbon and ketchup; simmer over medium heat, about 1 hour. Stir in wieners; simmer 15 minutes or until heated through. Pour into 2- to 3-quart slow cooker on low heat to keep warm.

10 to 12 servings.

Ethnic Discoveries

LUCILLE'S POLISH PRUNE COFFEE CAKE

Jayne Leight, Stacy, MN

DOUGH

5½ to 6½ cups all-purpose flour

3 tablespoons sugar

1 teaspoon salt

1 pkg. active dry yeast

1½ cups water

1½ cups whole milk

3 tablespoons butter

FILLING

3 cups pitted prunes

3 cups water

TOPPING

½ cup sugar

¾ cup all-purpose flour

⅓ cup butter

1 In large bowl, combine 2 cups flour, sugar, salt and yeast.

2 In medium saucepan, heat 1½ cups water, milk and butter over low heat until very warm (120° to 130°). Gradually pour liquid ingredients into dry ingredients and mix at low speed with electric mixer. Increase speed to medium and beat 2 minutes. Beat in ¾ cup flour and continue beating 2 more minutes, scraping bowl occasionally. Stir in enough flour, about 3 cups, to make soft dough. Turn dough onto lightly floured surface and knead until smooth and elastic, about 10 minutes. Shape into a ball and place in large greased bowl, turning over so that top of dough is greased. Cover with towel and let rise until doubled. Punch down dough by pushing center of dough; then push edges of dough into center. Let dough rise until doubled again.

3 Meanwhile, cook prunes and water 20 minutes in large saucepan; let cool. Mix together ½ cup sugar, ¾ cup flour and ⅓ cup butter in medium bowl until crumbly.

4 Heat oven to 400°F. Grease 2 (8x8-inch) cake pans. Cut dough in half and stretch over pan leaving some hanging over sides. Spoon half the filling in center of dough. Fold dough over filling. Sprinkle with half the topping. Repeat with second pan. Bake 40 minutes or until golden brown. If desired, use poppy seeds in place of prunes.

12 to 16 servings.

Lucille's Polish Prune Coffee Cake

CHICKEN CURRY INDIAN STYLE

Linette Britto, Germantown, MD

1 tablespoon olive oil

1 tablespoon clarified butter

1 large cinnamon stick

4 to 6 cloves

4 to 6 cardamom pods

2 bay leaves

Handful of fresh coriander leaves

Fresh mint leaves

2 onions, chopped

1 tablespoon ginger-garlic paste

3 to 4 green chiles

2 tomatoes, chopped

1½ teaspoons ground coriander

½ teaspoon ground cumin

1 teaspoon chili powder

¼ teaspoon turmeric

Salt, to taste

1 whole chicken (cut up)

❶ Heat oil and clarified butter in Dutch oven. Add cinnamon, cloves, cardamom, bay leaves, coriander leaves, mint and chopped onions; cook, stirring frequently, until golden brown. Add paste and continue cooking until mixture becomes slightly dark brown. Add chiles and tomatoes and cook an additional 2 minutes. Add coriander, cumin, chili powder, turmeric and salt; cook an additional 1 minute. Add chicken pieces, cover and cook until chicken is no longer pink in center and juices run clear. Sprinkle with lemon juice and serve with rice, if desired.

6 to 8 servings.

DANISH PUFF

Shirley Bosman, Kamloops, BC, Canada

1 cup butter, divided

2 cups all-purpose flour, divided

2 tablespoons water

1 cup water

1 teaspoon almond extract

3 eggs

Icing

Chopped almonds or nuts

❶ Heat oven to 350°F. Spray baking sheet with cooking spray.

❷ Cut ½ cup butter into 1 cup flour in large bowl. Mix water into flour mixture with fork; shape into a ball and divide in half. Pat into 2 (12x3-inch) strips on prepared baking sheet.

❸ Mix remaining butter and water in medium saucepan; bring to a boil. Remove from heat and add extract. Quickly stir in remaining flour until smooth. Stir in eggs, one at a time, beating well after each addition. Divide in half and spread evenly over each pastry strip. Bake 1 hour or until brown. Frost with icing and sprinkle with chopped nuts.

12 to 16 servings.

GREEK SALAD APPETIZER

Carol Stephan, Forest Park, IL

8 oz. crumbled feta cheese

4 oz. Greek olives, chopped

1 cup chopped tomato

6 anchovies, chopped

6 pepperoncini, chopped

4 green onions, sliced

2 tablespoons Greek dressing

❶ In large bowl, stir together feta cheese, olives, tomato, anchovies, pepperoncini, onions and Greek dressing. Refrigerate 30 minutes. Serve with pita chips.

10 to 12 servings.

HEARTY VEGETABLE SALAD

Dzhangirova Sveteana, Seattle, WA

4 tablespoons olive oil

1 cup finely chopped onion

1 (15-oz.) can kidney beans, drained and rinsed

4 pickled cucumbers, finely chopped

3 large carrots, peeled, cooked, finely chopped

2 large potatoes, peeled, cooked, chopped

1 large or 2 medium beets, peeled, cooked, finely chopped

1 cup sauerkraut, squeezed dry

3 tablespoons chopped fresh cilantro

3 tablespoons chopped fresh parsley

1/2 teaspoon ground coriander, if desired

Salt, to taste

Freshly ground pepper, to taste

1 In large skillet, heat oil over medium heat until hot. Add onion; cook until lightly browned.

2 Meanwhile, in large bowl, combine kidney beans, cucumbers, carrots, potatoes, beets, sauerkraut, cilantro, parsley, coriander, salt and pepper. Gently stir onion into vegetable mixture. Refrigerate until serving.

6 to 8 servings.

SWEET POTATO KUGEL

Sandy Ribiat, Southfield, MI

1 large can sweet potatoes or yams, drained

2 eggs

1/2 teaspoon ground cinnamon

1 1/2 teaspoons vanilla extract

1 Heat oven to 350°F. Spray 6x9-inch-deep baking dish with cooking spray. Mash sweet potatoes in large bowl until smooth. Stir in eggs, cinnamon and vanilla until well mixed and smooth. Pour potato mixture into prepared pan and bake 1 hour or until golden brown.

6 to 8 servings.

CHINATOWN SOY SAUCE CHICKEN

Celeste Ching, Honolulu, HI

1 cup water

1 whole star anise

3/4 cup soy sauce

1/2 cup packed dark brown sugar

1/4 cup dry sherry

1 tablespoon honey

4 garlic cloves, minced

3 slices fresh ginger, grated

3 1/2- to 4-lb. chicken

1 In covered Dutch oven, gently boil water and star anise 20 minutes.

2 In medium bowl, combine soy sauce, brown sugar, sherry, honey, garlic cloves and ginger. Add soy sauce mixture to Dutch oven; cover and bring to a boil. Reduce heat and simmer 5 minutes. Add chicken to Dutch oven and bring liquid back to a boil. Cover and reduce heat to low. Simmer, basting frequently, 15 minutes. Turn chicken and simmer, basting frequently, an additional 15 minutes. Turn breast side up, and cook until golden brown, another 15 minutes or until chicken is no longer pink in center and juices run clear. Remove chicken. Spoon 2 tablespoons cooking liquid onto plates and top with chicken.

4 servings.

Nopale Ensalada (Cactus Salad)

NOPALE ENSALADA (CACTUS SALAD)

Marie Ortiz, Tolleson, AZ

1 jar Nopales (cactus pads), drained and rinsed

1 (12-oz.) can pinto beans, drained

2 to 3 jalapeños or Serrano chiles, diced

1 small onion, diced

3 to 4 Roma tomatoes, diced

1 cucumber, peeled and diced

1 to 2 avocados, diced

1 small bunch fresh cilantro, chopped

1 to 2 small lemons

1 cup queso fresco cheese, grated or crumbled

1 In large serving bowl, gently stir together Nopales, pinto beans, chiles, onion, tomatoes, cucumber, avocados and cilantro. Squeeze fresh lemon juice over salad and stir gently to combine. Sprinkle cheese over salad.

10 to 12 servings.

POOR SOUP (POTATO CARAWAY)

Joy Smrcina, Cleveland, OH

4 cups chicken broth (or water with 2 to 4 bouillon cubes)

1 cup caraway seeds

5 to 6 medium-large potatoes, peeled and cubed

2 ribs celery, diced

½ small onion, diced

Handful chopped or shredded carrots

Salt, to taste

Freshly ground pepper, to taste

Flour roux (browned flour and butter), to thicken

1 Pour broth and caraway seeds into large saucepan; bring to a boil and boil 7 minutes. Add potatoes, vegetables, salt and pepper. Reduce heat to low and simmer until potatoes are tender. Whisk in enough roux to thicken. Simmer 15 minutes.

8 to 10 servings.

GERMAN APPLE PUFF

Beverly Dowdell, Westerville, OH

2 tablespoons butter, melted

3 Granny Smith apples, peeled, sliced

Honey, to taste

3 eggs

¾ cup all-purpose flour

¾ cup milk

2 tablespoons sugar

1 teaspoon baking powder

Cinnamon sugar

1 Heat oven to 400°F.

2 Pour butter into deep 9-inch pie pan. Place apples in pan and drizzle with honey. Stir together eggs, flour, milk, sugar and baking powder until smooth. Pour over apples. Sprinkle with cinnamon sugar; bake 30 minutes. Serve warm with syrup, if desired.

4 servings.

MRS. KATZ'S KOSHER MEATLOAF

Walt Stevenson, Topeka, KS

2 lbs. lean ground beef

1 cup matzo meal (unleavened cracker)

2 eggs

1 large onion, finely diced

4 garlic cloves, minced

1 teaspoon salt

¼ teaspoon white pepper

1 Heat oven to 375°F.

2 In large bowl, stir together beef, matzo meal, eggs, onion, garlic, salt and pepper until well blended; shape into a loaf. Bake in 13x9-inch baking dish until juices run clear when pierced. Let stand in oven 3 to 5 minutes before slicing.

6 to 8 servings.

GOLABKI (STUFFED CABBAGE)

Kathy Jacques, Chesterfield, MI

1 lb. ground beef

½ cup uncooked rice

1 cup bread crumbs

1 egg

1 small onion, minced

2 teaspoons salt

¾ teaspoon freshly ground pepper

1 to 2 large heads cabbage

½ cup milk

2 (10¾-oz.) cans condensed tomato soup

¼ cup ketchup

Mashed potatoes, if desired

Vegetables, if desired

1 Stir together beef, rice, bread crumbs, egg, onion, salt and pepper in large bowl. Bring water to a boil in large saucepan. Cut core from cabbage and submerge in boiling water. Let stand 10 minutes until leaves soften. Remove leaves and allow to cool slightly.

2 Place large tablespoon of meat mixture near top of each cabbage leaf; roll up and tuck sides in. Secure with toothpick.

3 Heat oven to 350°F. Spray Dutch oven with cooking spray and place cabbage rolls in bottom.

4 In medium bowl, stir together milk, soup and ketchup; pour over cabbage leaves, adding water if necessary. Cover and bake 2 to 3 hours or until tender. Serve with mashed potatoes and vegetables, if desired. Freeze rolls, if desired.

8 to 10 servings.

NASI GORENG (INDONESIAN FRIED RICE)

Shirley Bosman, Kamloops, BC, Canada

3 tablespoons vegetable oil

6 slices smoked bacon

1½ cups diced lean pork or chicken

1 medium onion, chopped

2 garlic cloves, crushed

1 medium carrot, shredded

2 cups cabbage, chopped

1 leek, cleaned, sliced

1 teaspoon trassi oedang, if desired (shrimp paste)

2 eggs, beaten

1 tablespoon ketjap manis (Indonesian soya sauce)

¼ teaspoon ground cumin or caraway seed

¼ teaspoon curcumae

½ teaspoon freshly ground pepper

¼ teaspoon ground coriander

1 teaspoon samal oelek or hot pepper sauce, if desired

Salt, to taste

1¾ cups long-grain rice, cooked according to package directions

1 In large skillet, heat oil over medium-high heat until hot. Add bacon and pork; fry bacon until cooked through. Stir in onion and garlic; reduce heat to medium and simmer 5 minutes.

2 Meanwhile, in large saucepan, cover carrot and cabbage with water and bring to a boil; boil 3 minutes and drain. Add leek and trassi oedang to meat mixture and cook 3 minutes. Stir in cooked cabbage mixture. Reduce heat to low and stir in eggs until thoroughly mixed. Add ketjap manis, ground cumin, curcumae, pepper, coriander, samal oelek and salt; stir to combine. Gently stir in rice.

4 to 6 servings.

SWEDISH BAKED RICE PUDDING

Alice Grove, Bethel, OH

½ cup long-grain rice

½ teaspoon salt

1 cinnamon stick or ½ teaspoon ground cinnamon

3 cups milk

3 eggs

½ to ¾ cup sugar

1½ cups cream or half-and-half

1 teaspoon vanilla extract

Cinnamon sugar

1 In double boiler, cook rice, salt and cinnamon and milk until rice is soft and most liquid has been absorbed, about 1 to 2 hours. Remove cinnamon stick and cool slightly.

2 In medium bowl, whisk together eggs and sugar; whisk in cream. Stir vanilla into rice. Slowly stir rice into egg mixture.

3 Heat oven to 400°F. Pour mixture into buttered 2- to 3-quart baking dish. Sprinkle with cinnamon sugar. Bake 20 minutes. Reduce heat to 325°F and bake until custard is set. Serve with fresh fruit and garnish with a cinnamon stick, if desired.

8 to 10 servings.

FRIED RED CABBAGE

Christiana L. Mendoza, Alamogordo, NM

½ head red cabbage, thinly sliced

1 garlic clove, crushed

1 Granny Smith apple, thinly sliced

1 bay leaf

2 to 3 tablespoons olive oil

1 to 2 tablespoons red wine vinegar

1 In large skillet, stir together red cabbage, garlic, apple, bay leaf and olive oil over medium heat until cabbage is soft. Add vinegar; cook until heated through. Remove and discard bay leaf. Serve with *Rouladen* (page 74).

6 to 8 servings.

PITA BREAD

Julie Cisler, Minneapolis, MN

1 teaspoon active dry yeast

1½ teaspoons sugar

1 cup warm water (110°F)

2 cups plus 1 tablespoon all-purpose flour

1 cup pastry flour

½ teaspoon salt

1 tablespoon applesauce

Olive oil, to taste

1 Dissolve yeast and sugar in small bowl in warm water.

2 In large bowl, combine all-purpose flour, pastry flour and salt. Stir in yeast mixture and apple-sauce; knead. If dough is too sticky, add flour, a tablespoon at a time, until desired consistency. Roll into a rope and cut into 8 pieces. Shape each piece into a ball and roll out into 6- to 8-inch circle.

3 For baked pita: Heat oven to 500°F and put dough circles on wire rack. Place in oven and bake 3 minutes or until the bread stops puffing up. Remove and carefully smash down the hot pita. To freeze, place pitas in plastic freezer bags.

4 For fried pita: In large skillet, heat olive oil over high heat. When almost smoking, place a dough circle in skillet; cook 1 to 2 minutes per side each side until brown spots begin to appear. Pita should look flat and resemble a tortilla when done. Repeat with remaining pitas. To freeze, place pitas in plastic freezer bags.

8 servings.

STOLLEN

Mable Watson, Lenoir, NC

FRUIT MIXTURE

$\frac{1}{3}$ cup raisins

$\frac{1}{3}$ cup toasted slivered almonds

$\frac{1}{3}$ cup candied cherries, chopped

$1\frac{1}{2}$ teaspoons all-purpose flour

$\frac{1}{2}$ recipe sweet dough (recipe below)

Powdered sugar

SWEET DOUGH

$3\frac{1}{2}$ to $4\frac{1}{2}$ cups all-purpose flour

$\frac{1}{3}$ cup sugar

2 pkgs. active dry yeast

$1\frac{1}{2}$ teaspoons salt

$\frac{1}{2}$ cup milk

$\frac{1}{4}$ cup water

$\frac{1}{4}$ cup butter

2 eggs, room temperature

1 For Fruit Mixture: In large bowl, combine raisins, almonds and cherries. Add flour; toss to coat.

2 For Sweet Dough: In large bowl, mix $1\frac{1}{2}$ cups flour, sugar, yeast and salt. In small saucepan, heat milk, water and butter until warm (110°F). Stir into flour mixture and beat until smooth. Beat in eggs one at a time. Gradually add flour until batter becomes too stiff to mix with a spoon or beater. Turn onto a lightly-floured cloth and work in enough flour to make a soft but firm dough. Knead until smooth and elastic, about 8 to 10 minutes.

3 Place dough in greased bowl and lightly grease the top. Cover with a cloth and let rise in warm (80° to 85°) place until doubled in bulk, about $1\frac{1}{2}$ hours.

4 On a lightly-floured cloth, knead fruit mixture into prepared dough until evenly distributed. Roll dough into 7x12-inch oval; fold in half lengthwise. Place on a greased baking sheet. Cover with a cloth and let rise in a warm (80° to 85°) place until almost double.

5 Heat oven to 350°F. Bake 25 minutes or until stollen is golden and sounds hollow when top is tapped with finger. Cool on a wire rack. Sprinkle with the powdered sugar.

Servings vary.

Stollen

PIEROGI (FILLED DUMPLINGS)

Kathy Jacques, Chesterfield, MI

PIEROGI DOUGH

4 medium potatoes, peeled, cooked, mashed

2 cups all-purpose flour

2 eggs

Salt, to taste

COTTAGE CHEESE FILLING

4 cups dry cottage cheese

Sugar to taste

¼ teaspoon ground cinnamon

Salt, to taste

1 egg

MASHED POTATO FILLING

3 cups mashed potatoes

1 cup shredded cheddar cheese

SAUERKRAUT FILLING

1 large can rinsed sauerkraut

½ small onion, chopped

1 Place potatoes in large bowl; stir in flour, eggs and salt. Knead until dough is formed. If dough is too soft, add additional flour if necessary. Dough will be the consistency of cookie dough. Roll dough and cut into dumplings using 3-inch cookie cutter.

2 Combine filling ingredients in 3 separate medium bowls. Place 1 tablespoon of each on cookie-shaped dumplings. Using a pastry brush, dampen edges with warm water; top with another dumpling. Press firmly with fingers to seal. Place in large saucepan of boiling salted water; boil 1 minute. Remove from water and brown in butter on both sides in large skillet or bake in buttered baking dish until browned on both sides. Serve with sour cream, if desired.

Servings vary.

ROULADEN (GERMAN STUFFED BEEF ROLLS)

Christiana L. Mendoza, Alamogordo, NM

4 to 6 teaspoons Dijon or German-style hot mustard

¼ cup thinly sliced onion, coarsely chopped

2½ lbs. top round or sirloin steak, trimmed and sliced ¼x4x8 inches

6 to 7 slices deli-cut Black Forest smoked ham

6 to 7 slices Gouda, Edam, Swiss, or provolone cheese

5 to 7 slices thick sliced bacon, cooked

3 to 4 dill pickles, sliced into ½-inch-thick slices

BROTH

1 cup water

1 cup red wine

1 (14½-oz.) can beef broth

1 cup chopped celery, optional

½ to ¾ cup sherry

¼ cup thinly sliced green onion

ROUX

1 tablespoon butter

2 tablespoons all-purpose flour

1 Spread mustard and onions over steak plate; top with slices of ham, cheese, bacon and pickles. Fold over ends and roll up jell-roll style. Tie with string or use toothpicks to secure. Heat the bacon drippings and add rolls, cook until browned on all sides; remove. Stir broth ingredients into skillet until well mixed. Add the rolls and simmer 45 minutes or until meat is tender. Remove rolls and set aside.

2 In small skillet, stir together butter and flour to make roux, cook until light brown and aroma is nutty. Whisk roux into broth; stir and cook several minutes to thicken. Add rolls and cook until heated through; serve with *Fried Red Cabbage* (page 71).

6 to 8 servings.

Main Attractions

CAJUN CEDAR SALMON

Dwight Bos, Omaha, NE

2 lbs. salmon fillet

3 tablespoons packed brown sugar

1 tablespoon freshly ground pepper

2 teaspoons chopped fresh or dried rosemary

½ teaspoon chili powder

½ teaspoon paprika

½ teaspoon salt

¼ teaspoon garlic powder

¼ teaspoon cayenne pepper

½ cup vinegar

1 Place salmon skin-side down on jelly-roll pan.

2 In small bowl, stir together brown sugar, pepper, rosemary, chili powder, paprika, salt, garlic powder and cayenne pepper. Brush salmon with vinegar and spread seasoning mixture over salmon; refrigerate 1 hour.

3 Meanwhile, soak a cedar plank in water 30 minutes, weighting down to submerge.

4 Heat grill. Remove salmon from marinade; discard marinade. Place salmon, skin-side down, on prepared plank and place plank on gas grill over medium-high heat or on charcoal grill 4 to 6 inches from medium-hot coals; cover grill. Sprinkle plank with water as needed during grilling. Grill 8 to 10 minutes per inch of thickness until top of fillet is golden brown and fish flakes easily with a fork. Remove skin before serving.

6 to 8 servings.

ASIAN SHRIMP

Squan Hopper, Manasquan, NJ

½ cup soy sauce

1 small piece fresh ginger, minced

1 small garlic clove, minced

½ teaspoon crushed red pepper

1½ tablespoons oyster sauce

Juice from ½ large orange

Dash chili-garlic sauce

Dash salt

1 lb. shelled, deveined, uncooked shrimp

1 In large bowl stir together soy sauce, ginger, garlic, red pepper, oyster sauce, orange juice, chili-garlic sauce and salt. Add shrimp and marinate in refrigerator 30 minutes.

2 Remove shrimp from marinade; discard marinade. Heat grill. Thread shrimp onto skewers and place on gas grill over medium heat or charcoal grill 4 to 6 inches from medium coals; cover grill and cook until shrimp turn pink.

4 servings.

MAYFLOWER LOAF

Jude Lindner, Homeland, CA

1 (11- to 15-oz.) can mixed vegetables

⅓ cup dried bread crumbs

1 egg, beaten

1 lb. ground beef

⅓ cup finely chopped onion

½ teaspoon seasoned salt

⅛ teaspoon freshly ground pepper

1 Heat oven to 375°F. Drain vegetables saving 3 tablespoons liquid. In large bowl, combine bread crumbs, egg, ground beef, onion, salt and pepper. Add liquid from vegetables and form into 9x12-inch rectangle. Sprinkle with vegetables. Roll up meat jelly-roll style and set in large baking pan, seam-side down. Bake 35 to 40 minutes or until beef is no longer pink. Cool slightly before slicing.

4 servings.

Asian Shrimp

CHERYL'S CHICKEN AND ARTICHOKES

Cheryl Echevarria, Bentwood, NY

3 tablespoons bacon grease

4 chicken thighs or drumsticks

Salt, to taste

Freshly ground pepper, to taste

1½ lbs. small red-skinned potatoes, unpeeled, halved

4 large garlic cloves, minced

¾ cup dry white wine

¾ cup chicken broth

½ cup raisins, if desired

1½ teaspoons dried oregano

1 teaspoon dried thyme

8 oz. frozen artichoke hearts, thawed

2 tablespoons unsalted butter

1 Heat oven to 450°F.

2 In large ovenproof saucepan or Dutch oven, heat bacon grease over medium-high heat. Sprinkle chicken with salt and pepper. Add chicken to saucepan; cook until golden brown on both sides, in batches if necessary, about 10 minutes. Remove chicken from saucepan.

3 Cook potatoes in same saucepan until golden brown, stirring occasionally, about 10 minutes. Stir in garlic and sauté 1 minute. Pour in wine and scrape up any brown bits on the bottom of pan. Add broth, raisins, oregano, thyme and chicken; stir to combine. Bring to a boil over medium-high heat. Cover and bake until chicken is no long pink, about 20 minutes.

4 Transfer chicken to a platter; arrange potatoes around chicken. Return pan to medium heat and add artichoke hearts. Cover and simmer until tender, stirring often, about 4 minutes. Reduce heat; stir in butter until melted. Pour sauce over chicken and potatoes to serve.

4 servings.

CHUCK'S CHUCK ROAST

Charles Widbin, St. Louis, MO

8 to 10 slices thick-cut, maple-cured bacon

3- to 4-lb. beef chuck roast

¼ cup minced garlic

1 tablespoon freshly ground pepper

1 tablespoon kosher (coarse) salt

¼ cup Riesling white wine, if desired

1 Heat oven to 275°F.

2 Line 13x9-inch pan with 4 to 5 slices of bacon.

3 Lay roast on bacon and sprinkle with garlic, pepper and salt. Put 1 slice of bacon on each end of the roast and lay 3 to 4 slices across the top of the roast. Use toothpicks to attach bacon to roast if necessary. Pour wine into bottom of roasting pan. Bake 2 to 2½ hours or until roast is desired doneness. Cover loosely with aluminum foil and let sit 20 minutes before slicing. Slice into ⅛-inch-thick slices and serve with bacon.

8 to 12 servings.

ITALIAN CHICKEN

Renee Felkins, Thatcher, AZ

6 boneless skinless chicken breast halves

1 cup Italian dressing

6 tablespoons pesto

6 slices mozzarella cheese

½ cup sliced black olives, if desired

1 avocado, sliced, if desired

1 Place chicken in a large re-sealable plastic bag and pour in dressing. Refrigerate at least 1 hour. Remove chicken from marinade; discard marinade.

2 Heat grill. Place chicken on gas grill over medium heat or on charcoal grill 4 to 6 inches from medium coals; cover grill and cook 6 to 8 minutes or until chicken is no longer pink and juices run clear. Top each chicken breast with a tablespoon of pesto and a cheese slice. Cook an additional 1 to 2 minutes, until cheese is melted. Garnish with black olives or sliced avocado.

6 servings.

CURRY CHOPS

Shelly Goodwin, Tonto Basin, AZ

1 (16-oz.) bag frozen hash browns

Salt, to taste

Freshly ground pepper, to taste

8 tablespoons butter, melted

Curry, to taste

4 to 6 bone-in or boneless pork chops

1 medium onion, thinly sliced

1 Heat oven to 350°F.

2 Place hash browns in large bowl and sprinkle with salt, pepper and half of the butter. Cook hash browns in large skillet over medium-high heat until golden brown.

3 Place pork chops in 13x9-inch baking dish and sprinkle with salt, pepper and curry. Top with onions and hash browns, browned-side up. Sprinkle with remaining melted butter. Bake 1 hour or until pork chops are cooked through and potatoes are deep golden brown.

4 to 6 servings.

PEANUT BUTTER PORK CHOPS

Barbara A. Lindsey, West Warren, MA

6 bone-in pork chops

1 (10¾-oz.) can condensed cream of mushroom soup

1 can milk

2 tablespoons creamy peanut butter

1 to 2 tablespoons Worcestershire sauce

1 large onion, sliced

1 In large skillet, cook pork chops over medium-high heat until browned.

2 Meanwhile, stir together mushroom soup, milk, peanut butter and Worcestershire sauce in medium bowl. Top each browned pork chop with onion slice and then soup mixture. Cover and let simmer one hour. Serve with white rice, if desired.

6 servings.

EGGPLANT SLICES WITH TOMATOES

Dzhangirova Sveteana, Seattle, WA

1 large eggplant (about 1 lb.)

1½ teaspoons salt, divided

4 tablespoons olive oil, divided

2 to 3 large tomatoes, sliced ¼ inch thick

1 red, yellow or orange bell pepper, thinly sliced

3 garlic cloves, minced

2 tablespoons finely chopped fresh cilantro

¼ teaspoon freshly ground pepper

1 Cut eggplant crosswise into ¼-inch-thick slices. Place in large baking dish and sprinkle with 1 teaspoon salt. Let stand 15 to 20 minutes; rinse and pat dry.

2 In large skillet, heat 3 tablespoons olive oil over medium-high heat until hot. Add eggplant slices; reduce heat and fry until light golden brown and softened, turning once. Remove to serving platter.

3 Add remaining 1 tablespoon olive oil to skillet and cook tomato slices, turning once. Top eggplant with tomato slices and bell pepper.

4 In small bowl, stir together garlic and cilantro; sprinkle over bell peppers. Season with additional salt and pepper.

4 servings.

Kielbasa Pan Roast

KIELBASA PAN ROAST

Christina L. Mendoza, Alamogordo, NM

4 slices bacon, cut into 1-inch pieces

1 large carrot, peeled, thinly sliced, about 1 cup

1 lb. small red potatoes, unpeeled, sliced, about 2 cups

Small bunch broccoli, cut into 2-inch pieces, about 2 cups

1 medium onion, halved, sliced, about 1 cup

½ teaspoon dried marjoram, coarsely crushed

Salt, to taste

Freshly ground pepper, to taste

1 lb. kielbasa sausage, cut into ½-inch-thick slices

¾ cup water

1 In large skillet, cook bacon until crisp over medium heat; remove with slotted spoon and drain on paper towels. Add vegetables and seasonings to skillet and cook 5 minutes, stirring often, until softened. Add kielbasa and water. Cover and cook an additional 15 to 20 minutes, stirring occasionally, until potatoes and carrots are tender. Crumble bacon over kielbasa mixture before serving. Serve with biscuits, if desired.

4 to 6 servings.

STEAK MARINATE

Mary Arredondo, Billings, MT

1 tablespoon steak seasoning

1 tablespoon packed brown sugar

1 teaspoon onion powder

½ teaspoon dried oregano leaves

¼ cup olive oil

4 (6-oz.) steaks

1 In large re-sealable plastic bag, combine seasoning, brown sugar, onion powder, oregano and olive oil. Add steaks; shake to coat. Refrigerate at least 2 hours. Remove steaks from rub; discard rub.

2 Heat grill. Place steaks on gas grill over medium heat or on charcoal grill 4 to 6 inches from medium coals; cover grill. Cook steaks 6 to 8 minutes or until desired doneness.

4 servings.

FRENCH ONION SALISBURY STEAK

Elaine Eddleman, Arnold, MO

1¼ lbs. ground beef

¼ cup chopped fresh parsley

2 tablespoons green onion, thinly sliced

1¾ teaspoons salt, divided

½ teaspoon freshly ground pepper

¼ teaspoon dried sage

2 tablespoons all-purpose flour

1 tablespoon vegetable oil

2 cups sliced onions

1 teaspoon sugar

1 tablespoon minced garlic

1 tablespoon tomato paste

2 cups beef broth

¼ cup dry red wine

½ teaspoon dried thyme

1 recipe *Cheese Toasts* (page 83)

4 teaspoons chopped fresh parsley

4 teaspoons freshly shredded Parmesan cheese

1 In large bowl, combine ground beef, parsley, onion, 1 teaspoon salt, pepper and sage. Divide evenly into 4 oval patties, each ¾ to 1 inch thick.

2 Place flour in shallow dish; dredge each patty in flour, reserving remaining flour.

3 In large skillet, heat oil over medium heat. Add patties; cook until browned, about 3 minutes per side. Remove patties from skillet.

4 Add onions and sugar to skillet; cook 5 minutes, stirring occasionally. Stir in garlic and tomato paste; cook 1 minute or until paste begins to brown. Sprinkle with reserved flour; cook 1 minute. Stir in broth, wine, remaining salt and thyme. Return patties to skillet and bring to a boil. Reduce heat to medium-low, cover and simmer 10 minutes until patties are no longer pink in center. Serve steaks on Cheese Toasts with sauce ladled over. Garnish with parsley and Parmesan cheese.

4 servings.

SHELLY'S PORK TENDERLOIN WITH 7-SPICE PORK RUB

Shelly Goodwin, Tonto Basin, AZ

½ teaspoon garlic powder

½ teaspoon freshly ground pepper

½ teaspoon onion powder

½ teaspoon garlic salt

½ teaspoon curry power

½ teaspoon dried ground sage

¼ teaspoon ground cardamom

1-lb. pork tenderloin, boneless

2 tablespoons olive oil

1 In small bowl, stir together garlic powder, pepper, onion powder, garlic salt, curry powder, sage and cardamom.

2 Rub pork with oil and then spice rub. Place in large re-sealable plastic bag and refrigerate overnight. Remove pork from marinade; discard marinade.

3 Heat oven to 350°F. Bake 45 minutes to 1 hour or until pork reaches an internal temperature of 160°F. Remove from oven and let rest 5 minutes. Slice into ½- to 1-inch-thick slices.

4 to 6 servings.

EASY ROAST

Karen Davidson, Purdy, MO

1 (10¾-oz.) can cream of mushroom soup

1 (12-oz.) can cola

1 pkg. French onion soup mix

3- to 4-lb. beef or pork roast

1 Heat oven to 350°F. In 4- to 5-quart baking dish, stir together soup, cola and soup mix. Add meat; bake 3 hours or until meat is fork-tender. Serve with rice and vegetables, if desired.

8 to 12 servings.

SULTRY PORK CHOP CURRY

Heidi Walker, Independence, MO

2 to 4 tablespoons extra-virgin olive oil

4 to 6 pork or lamb chops, 4 to 6 oz. each

½ cup water

½ (12-oz.) bottle teriyaki sauce

½ cup red wine

1 teaspoon curry powder

1 teaspoon freshly grated ginger

1 (1½-oz.) box raisins or currants

2 to 3 garlic cloves, minced

Dash soy sauce

1 In large skillet, heat olive oil over medium-high heat until hot. Add pork chops; cook until browned on both sides and no longer pink in center.

2 Meanwhile, in small bowl, whisk together water, teriyaki sauce and wine. Sprinkle pork with curry and ginger. Pour raisins and garlic into skillet. Cover and simmer 3 minutes. Pour in sauce; cover and cook 4 to 5 minutes. Uncover and simmer until sauce thickens. Serve pork topped with raisin sauce.

4 to 6 servings.

SHORT RIBS OR BRISKET

Ann Miller, Los Angeles, CA

2 onions, sliced or chopped

3 to 4 lbs. beef brisket or short ribs

½ large bottle A-1 sauce

Cooked potatoes, if desired

Cooked miniature onions, if desired

1 Heat oven to 325°F.

2 Place sliced onions on bottom of large baking dish. Top onions with meat and A-1 sauce; cover and bake until meat is fork-tender. Remove meat from sauce and refrigerate overnight. Skim off fat. Slice brisket and cover with sauce; reheat. If needed add water for more gravy. Serve meat with sauce.

8 to 10 servings.

TERIYAKI BACON-WRAPPED TURKEY WINGS

Debbie Mitchem, Panama City, FL

½ cup teriyaki basting sauce and marinade

2 tablespoons soy sauce

3 turkey wings, cut at joints

Bacon, to taste

Salt, to taste

Freshly ground pepper, to taste

Dried oregano, to taste

1 Heat oven to 325°F.

2 In small bowl, stir together teriyaki and soy sauce.

3 Wrap each turkey wing with enough bacon to completely cover wing. Place wings on broiler pan; sprinkle with salt, pepper and oregano and brush top side with teriyaki mixture. Cook 20 minutes; turn wings and baste. Continue turning and basting until wings are done, about 45 minutes. Turn oven to low broil and cook until wings are no longer pink in center and bacon is browned. Turn and repeat. Remove and let stand 5 minutes before serving.

4 to 6 servings.

CHEESE TOASTS

Elaine Eddleman, Arnold, MO

4 slices French bread

2 tablespoons unsalted butter, melted

½ teaspoon garlic powder

Dash paprika

¼ cup shredded Swiss or mozzarella cheese

1 Heat oven 400°F. Spray baking sheet with cooking spray. Place bread on baking sheet. In small bowl, combine butter, garlic powder and paprika; spread mixture over top side of bread and sprinkle with cheese. Bake until bread is crisp and cheese is bubbling, about 10 to 15 minutes.

4 servings.

YOGURT ROASTED CHICKEN

Brenda T. Brooks, Greenbelt, MD

2 cups plain yogurt

4 garlic cloves, crushed

1 teaspoon ground ginger

2 teaspoons paprika

Salt, to taste

2 teaspoons white pepper

4 tablespoons chopped fresh parsley

1 medium onion, chopped

4- to 5-lb. chicken, quartered

1 In large bowl, stir together yogurt, garlic, ginger, paprika, salt, pepper, parsley and onion.

2 Place chicken in 13x9-inch glass baking dish and spread yogurt mixture over chicken; cover and let chicken refrigerate 3 hours or overnight.

3 Heat oven to 350°F. Bake, uncovered, 2 hours or until cooked through and golden brown, basting often with sauce. Serve with rice or noodles, buttered and steamed carrots and wheat bread, if desired.

4 to 6 servings.

MINI MEAT LOAVES

Maggie Martinez, Minnetonka, MN

½ cup dried bread crumbs

¼ cup barbecue sauce

¼ cup onion, chopped, if desired

1 egg

1½ lbs. lean ground beef

Ketchup

1 Heat oven to 375°F.

2 In large bowl, combine bread crumbs, barbecue sauce, onion, egg and ground beef until well mixed. Divide mixture evenly into 6 ungreased muffin cups. Top with ketchup. Bake 18 to 20 minutes or until meat is no longer pink.

6 servings.

GARLIC SALMON
A LA BLANC

Thu Blackwell, Roosevelt, UT

1 lb. fresh salmon fillets

2 to 3 garlic cloves, minced

Salt, to taste

Freshly ground pepper, to taste

1 cup diced Italian plum tomatoes

¼ cup Sauvignon Blanc or dry white wine

1 teaspoon dried basil

1 cup shredded Swiss cheese

1 Heat oven to 350°F. Cover baking sheet with aluminum foil.

2 Place salmon on prepared sheet and sprinkle with garlic, salt, pepper and diced tomatoes. Pour wine over salmon and sprinkle with dried basil. Bake 15 minutes and sprinkle cheese over salmon. Bake an additional 3 to 5 minutes or until cheese is melted and salmon flakes easily with a fork.

2 to 3 servings.

SALISBURY STEAK WITH
MUSHROOM GRAVY

Jude Lindner, Homeland, CA

1 lb. ground beef

½ small onion, finely chopped

1 egg

¼ cup dried bread crumbs

1 tablespoon seasoned salt

1 (10¾-oz.) can cream of mushroom soup

1 cup milk

1 In large bowl, combine beef, onion, egg, bread crumbs and salt. Shape mixture into patties; cook in large skillet over medium heat until browned on both sides. In medium bowl, stir together soup and milk. Pour soup mixture over patties in skillet. Lower heat, cover and cook an additional 20 minutes or until patties are no longer pink in center.

4 servings.

BEER AND CHILI
BRAISED SHORT RIBS

Brian Redman, Louisville, KY

5 lbs. short ribs

Salt, to taste

Freshly ground pepper, to taste

¼ cup vegetable oil

½ cup diced onion

½ cup diced tomato

¼ cup diced celery

¼ cup diced carrots

¼ cup diced poblano chile

4 garlic cloves, crushed

1 teaspoon ground cumin

1 teaspoon ground chipotle chiles

1 teaspoon paprika

1 teaspoon ground ancho chiles

¼ cup all-purpose flour

2 cans beer

2 cups beef broth

1 Heat oven to 300°F.

2 Sprinkle short ribs with salt and pepper. In roasting pan, heat oil over medium-high heat until hot. Add ribs; cook until browned on all sides. Remove ribs from pan.

3 Add onion, tomato, celery, carrots, poblano chile, garlic, cumin, chipotle chiles, paprika and ancho chiles to pan; cook, stirring frequently, until vegetables are tender. Stir in flour; cook until well blended. Pour in beer and broth and bring to a boil, stirring constantly until thickened. Return ribs to roasting pan; cover with foil and bake 4 hours. Serve ribs and sauce over mashed potatoes and a side of green beans, if desired.

4 to 6 servings.

Beer and Chili Braised Short Ribs

ITALIAN MEATBALLS

Cindy Thompson, Chicago, IL

MEATBALLS

2 lbs. lean ground beef

2 lbs. ground pork

3 eggs, lightly beaten

4 to 6 garlic cloves, minced

1½ cups freshly grated Parmesan or Romano cheese

1 cup dried Italian bread crumbs

1 cup whole milk ricotta cheese

1 teaspoon crushed red pepper

1 tablespoon dried oregano

2 tablespoons dried basil

6 drops hot pepper sauce

SAUCE

¼ cup olive oil

1½ cups chopped sweet onion

4 garlic cloves, minced

2 (32-oz.) jars tomato-basil pasta sauce

1 (14½-oz.) can diced tomatoes, undrained

1 (6-oz.) can tomato paste

½ tablespoon dried oregano

½ tablespoon dried basil

½ cup freshly grated Parmesan or Romano cheese

Salt, to taste

Freshly ground pepper, to taste

1 For Meatballs: In large bowl, gently combine ground beef, ground pork, eggs, garlic, Parmesan cheese, bread crumbs, ricotta cheese, crushed red pepper, oregano, basil and hot pepper sauce. Scoop or shape mixture into 2-tablespoon-size meatballs. Set aside.

2 For Sauce: In large saucepan or Dutch oven, heat oil over medium heat. Add onions; cook until crisp-tender, about 3 minutes. Add meatballs, in batches if necessary, and cook until browned and no longer pink in center, turning occasionally, about 10 minutes. Remove meatballs to paper towels. Add garlic, pasta sauce, tomatoes, tomato paste, oregano, basil, Parmesan cheese, salt and pepper to saucepan; mix well, scraping up any browned bits. Return meatballs to sauce. Turn heat to low and simmer about 30 minutes to blend flavors.

10 to 12 servings.

One Dish Meals

BRUNCH CASSEROLE

Maryellen Scheel, Hazelwood, MO

1 box seasoned croutons

1½ to 2 lbs. combination of cooked meats such as sausage, ham and/or bacon

6 eggs

2 cups milk

1 (10¾-oz.) can cream of mushroom soup

2 cups freshly grated cheese

4 oz. sliced mushrooms

Salt, to taste

Freshly ground pepper, to taste

Chopped peppers, if desired

Chopped onion, if desired

Hot pepper sauce, to taste

❶ Spray 13x9-inch baking dish with cooking spray.

❷ Place croutons in bottom of prepared baking dish. Sprinkle cooked meat over croutons.

❸ In large bowl, combine eggs, milk, mushroom soup, 1 cup of the cheese, mushrooms, salt and pepper. Pour mixture over meat and top with remaining 1 cup of cheese. Refrigerate overnight.

❹ Heat oven to 325°F. Bake 1 hour or until eggs are cooked through.

10 to 12 servings.

CHICKEN MOZZARELLA CASSEROLE

Jennifer Elliot, Plainfield, IL

2 (10¾-oz.) cans cream of chicken, mushroom or celery soup

½ cup white or red wine, if desired

4 boneless skinless chicken breast halves, cubed

1 to 1½ cups shredded mozzarella cheese

8 oz. broccoli, peas or spinach, if desired

8 oz. stuffing, cooked according to package directions

❶ Heat oven to 350°F. Spray 3- to 4-quart baking dish with cooking spray.

❷ In large bowl, mix soup and wine. Place cubed chicken in bottom of prepared baking dish. Sprinkle with cheese and vegetables. Pour soup mixture over vegetables and top with stuffing. Bake 30 to 45 minutes or until chicken is no longer pink.

4 to 6 servings.

GREEN BEANS AND SAUCE

Susan Pacenza, Nineveh, NY

1 lb. fresh green beans, cleaned

1 lb. ground beef

1 onion, chopped

1 garlic clove, crushed

1 (28-oz.) can tomato puree or crushed tomatoes

4 medium potatoes, peeled, chopped

Salt, to taste

Freshly ground pepper, to taste

❶ Blanch green beans for 1 minute in boiling water; drain.

❷ In large saucepan, cook ground beef, onion and garlic over medium heat until beef is no longer pink; drain. Stir in pureed tomatoes, equal amount of water, potatoes, green beans, salt and pepper. Simmer until potatoes are tender and sauce is thickened. Serve with Italian bread and salad, if desired.

6 to 8 servings.

BRUNCH PUFF

Hope Wasylenki, Gahanna, OH

16 slices bread, crusts removed if desired

2 cups diced ham, chicken or turkey or 1 lb.
cooked and drained sausage

1 medium sweet onion, diced, about 1 cup

2 cups shredded cheese of choice, divided

6 eggs, beaten

3 cups milk

$\frac{1}{2}$ teaspoon salt

$\frac{1}{2}$ teaspoon dry mustard

1 teaspoon dried parsley

1 cup crushed potato chips, cracker crumbs
or croutons

$\frac{1}{2}$ cup melted butter

1 Spray 13x9-inch pan with cooking spray.

2 Layer 8 slices of bread, meat, onion, 1 cup of
cheese, remaining 8 slices of bread and cheese.

3 In large bowl, stir together eggs, milk. salt, mustard and parsley; pour over bread and refrigerate,
covered, overnight.

4 Heat oven to 350°F. Remove cover; top with
crushed chips, crackers or croutons and drizzle
with butter. Bake 1 hour or until cooked through.
Serve with salad and fruit, if desired.

6 to 10 servings.

CHICKEN CREAM ENCHILADAS

Jodi Paige Walker, Tucson, AZ

2 tablespoons butter

2 large onions, thinly sliced, about 2 cups

2 cups diced, cooked chicken

$\frac{1}{2}$ cup chopped roasted sweet red pepper,
from jar

2 (3-oz.) pkgs. cream cheese, cubed, softened

Salt, to taste

Freshly ground pepper, to taste

12 corn tortillas

$\frac{2}{3}$ cup whipping cream

2 cups shredded Pepper Jack cheese

Sliced olives

Chopped fresh cilantro

Lime wedges

1 Heat oven to 375°F.

2 Heat large, deep skillet over medium heat. Add
butter and onions to skillet; cook, stirring occasionally, about 20 minutes or until onions are softened and just beginning to brown. Remove from
heat and stir in chicken, sweet pepper, cream
cheese, salt and pepper. Spoon about $\frac{1}{3}$ cup of
chicken mixture down center of each tortilla and
roll to enclose.

3 Place enchiladas, seam-side down in 13x9-inch
baking dish. Brush tops of enchiladas with whipping cream and sprinkle evenly with cheese. Bake,
uncovered, 20 minutes or until heated. Garnish
with olives, cilantro and lime wedges, if desired.

6 servings.

CHICKEN ENCHILADAS

Naomi J. Rauscher, Sacramento, CA

1 whole chicken, cooked, skin and bones removed, shredded

1 (4½-oz.) can diced green chiles

1 (4½-oz.) can green chili salsa

1 teaspoon salt

2 cups sour cream

2 to 3 tablespoons vegetable oil

12 to 18 corn tortillas

8 oz. shredded Monterey Jack cheese

Olives, if desired

1 Heat oven to 425°F.

2 In large bowl, combine chicken, green chiles and chili salsa.

3 In small bowl, stir salt into sour cream.

4 In large skillet, heat oil over medium-high heat until hot. Add tortillas; cook 1 to 2 minutes per side. Spread 1 teaspoon sour cream onto tortilla and top with chicken mixture; roll up. Place tortillas in 13x9-inch baking dish. Continue rolling enchiladas until chicken mixture is used up. Spread remaining sour cream over the tops of the enchiladas and sprinkle with cheese and olives, if desired. Bake until cheese is melted and golden brown.

6 to 8 servings.

BREAKFAST PIZZA

Mary Beth Hogan, Frisco, TX

PIZZA

1-lb. loaf frozen bread dough, thawed

3 eggs

¼ cup milk

Salt, to taste

Freshly ground pepper, to taste

½ cup shredded cheddar cheese

½ cup shredded three-cheese blend

TOPPINGS

Cooked diced bacon, to taste

Cooked diced sausage, to taste

Chopped bell peppers, to taste

Chopped onions, to taste

Chopped mushrooms, to taste

Chopped tomatoes, to taste

1 Heat oven to 350°F. Brush pizza stone with olive oil; heat in oven 5 minutes. Spread thawed bread onto pizza stone.

2 In medium bowl, whisk together eggs, milk, salt, pepper and cheddar cheese. Spread mixture onto dough and sprinkle with cheese blend. Top with desired toppings. Bake 20 to 25 minutes. Cut into slices to serve.

6 to 8 servings.

Breakfast Pizza

DANISH CASSEROLE

Trouble O'Hara, Colorado Springs, CO

1 cup uncooked elbow macaroni

1 lb. ground beef

1 egg

5 slices bread, crusts removed, coarsely chopped

1½ teaspoons salt, divided

¼ teaspoon freshly ground pepper

3 eggs, separated

¾ cup milk

¼ cup minced red pepper

1 tablespoon butter, melted

1 cup shredded cheddar cheese

¼ cup shredded Monterey Jack cheese

3 oz. crumbled blue cheese

1 Heat oven to 350°F.

2 Cook macaroni according to package directions.

3 In large bowl, stir together beef, whole egg, 2 bread slices, 1 teaspoon salt and pepper. Press mixture evenly into bottom of 10-inch fluted pie plate.

4 In another large bowl, stir together egg yokes, milk, 3 crumpled bread slices, ½ teaspoon salt, bell pepper, butter, cheeses and macaroni.

5 In small bowl, beat egg whites until stiff and fold into macaroni mixture. Pour mixture over meat in pie pan. Bake, uncovered, 50 to 60 minutes until top is lightly brown and beef is no longer pink.

8 servings.

CREAMY CHICKEN WITH STUFFING

Crystal Harris, Corpus Christi, TX

4 boneless skinless chicken breast halves

4 slices Swiss or Monterey Jack cheese

1 (10¾-oz.) can cream of chicken soup

¼ cup dry white wine or low-sodium chicken broth

½ cup herb seasoned stuffing

¼ cup butter, melted

1 Heat oven to 350°F. Spray 13x9-inch baking dish with cooking spray.

2 Arrange chicken in prepared dish and top with one slice of cheese.

3 In small bowl, whisk together soup and wine. Spoon soup mixture evenly over chicken and sprinkle with stuffing mix. Drizzle melted butter over stuffing. Bake, uncovered, 45 to 55 minutes or until chicken is no longer pink.

4 servings.

SAUER POTATO BAKE

Mike Christenson, Elk River, MN

3 large potatoes, unpeeled, thinly sliced

1 medium onion, halved crosswise, cut into wedges

½ of (1-oz.) pkg. onion soup mix

1 lb. sausage in casing, cut into 1-inch pieces

1 (15¾-oz.) can sauerkraut, drained, rinsed

4 tablespoons butter

1 Heat oven to 375°F.

2 Place potatoes and onion in large bowl. Sprinkle with soup mix. Pour into 13x9-inch baking pan; top with sausage and sauerkraut. Dot with butter. Cover and bake 45 minutes to 1 hour until sausage is cooked through.

4 to 6 servings.

EASY BEEF STEW

Jaimie Frattolillo, Glassboro, NJ

6 medium russet potatoes, peeled, cut into
1/2-inch pieces

1 onion, cut into thin wedges

Salt, to taste

Freshly ground pepper, to taste

1/2 tablespoon onion powder

1/2 tablespoon garlic powder

1/2 tablespoon dried basil

1 to 2 tablespoons vegetable oil, divided

1 lb. beef stew meat

2 garlic cloves, minced

1 (1- to 3-oz.) pkg. dry beef gravy mix

1 (15-oz.) can peas, drained

1 (6-oz.) can mushroom pieces and
stems, drained

1 Heat oven to 350°F. Spray 13x9-inch baking pan
with cooking spray.

2 Place potatoes and onions in prepared pan;
sprinkle with salt, pepper, onion powder, garlic
powder, basil and 1 tablespoon oil. Bake 1 hour,
stirring halfway through.

3 Meanwhile heat remaining tablespoon oil in
large skillet over medium-high heat; cook beef
with garlic until browned; stir in gravy packet and
water amount indicated on package directions. Stir
in peas and mushrooms; bring to a boil. Reduce
heat and simmer 15 minutes. Place potatoes in
individual bowls and pour meat mixture over
them. Serve with sourdough bread, if desired.

6 to 8 servings.

FIREHOUSE SPAGHETTI

Karin B. Schlenker, Powell, TN

2 tablespoons vegetable oil

1 medium onion, diced

2 large garlic cloves

1 (14.5-oz.) can diced tomatoes with green chiles
or jalapeño peppers

2 (8-oz.) cans unsalted tomato sauce

1 (7-oz.) can unsalted mushroom stems and
pieces, drained

1/2 teaspoon dried oregano

1 teaspoon dried basil

Dash crushed red pepper

Dash dried marjoram

Hot pepper sauce, to taste

Salt, to taste

Freshly ground pepper, to taste

1 (16-oz.) pkg. spaghetti

Freshly grated Parmesan cheese, to taste

1 In large saucepan, heat oil over medium-high
heat until hot. Add onion and garlic; cook until
softened. Stir in diced tomatoes, tomato sauce,
mushrooms, oregano, basil, red pepper, marjoram,
hot pepper sauce, salt and pepper; cover and let
simmer 10 to 15 minutes, stirring occasionally until
heated through.

2 Meanwhile, cook spaghetti according to package
directions. Spoon sauce over spaghetti and serve
with grated Parmesan cheese. Serve with a green
salad with oil and vinegar dressing and garlic
bread, if desired.

4 servings.

HONG KONG HAMBURGER

Shirley Bosman, Kamloops, BC, Canada

PINEAPPLE GLAZE

⅓ cup brown sugar

2 teaspoons cornstarch

1 large can sliced pineapple, drained, ¼ cup juice reserved

3 tablespoons vinegar

1 tablespoon Worcestershire sauce

1 tablespoon soy sauce

SANDWICH

1 lb. ground beef

1 egg, beaten

½ teaspoon salt

Dash freshly ground pepper

½ (1-lb.) loaf French bread, sliced in half horizontally

1 green pepper, sliced into rings

Cherry tomatoes, if desired

1 chopped onion or ½ pkg. onion soup mix, optional

1 In large saucepan, stir together brown sugar, cornstarch and pineapple syrup, vinegar, Worcestershire sauce and soy sauce. Cook and stir constantly until mixture thickens and comes to a boil.

2 Heat oven to broil. Combine ground beef, egg, salt and pepper in large bowl. Spread meat mixture evenly over bottom half of bread, spreading mixture to edges. Place on broiler rack 4 to 6 inches from heat source. Broil 12 to 15 minutes. Brush meat with pineapple glaze and top with pineapple slices, green pepper and tomatoes. Brush with remaining glaze; return to oven and broil 3 minutes until topping is heated and meat is cooked through.

6 to 8 servings.

MEDITERRANEAN CRESCENT ROLL PIZZA

Meghan Sidelnick, Salunga, PA

1 (10-oz.) pkg. crescent rolls

1 tablespoon olive oil

2 finely diced roasted red bell peppers (from a jar)

¼ cup chopped black olives

¼ cup finely chopped artichoke hearts

1 (8-oz.) bag shredded mozzarella cheese

Dried oregano, if desired

Dried basil, if desired

Crushed red pepper, if desired

1 Heat oven to 375°F.

2 Roll crescent rolls onto pizza pan or baking stone, pressing seams firmly. Drizzle olive oil over dough and bake 7 to 10 minutes or until golden brown; cool slightly. Top with bell peppers, olives, artichoke hearts, mozzarella cheese, oregano, basil and crushed red pepper; bake an additional 10 minutes or until cheese is melted.

6 to 8 servings.

MISSIONARY SUPPER

Carl Boutilier, Freeport, OH

1 cup yogurt

1 cup sour cream or cottage cheese

½ cup chopped fruit

½ cup nuts, if desired

2 cups cooked oatmeal

1 In large bowl, mix together yogurt, sour cream, fruit and nuts. Divide oatmeal between 2 serving bowls and top with yogurt mixture.

2 servings.

LASAGNA FLORENTINE

Cora Raiford, Jacksonville, FL

2 (10-oz.) pkgs. frozen chopped spinach, thawed, drained and squeezed dry

1 large carrot, shredded

1 large zucchini, shredded

½ cup minced onion

Basil, to taste

Oregano, to taste

¼ teaspoon ground nutmeg

1 large garlic clove, minced

½ cup egg substitute or 2 whole eggs

1 (2-lb.) container low-fat ricotta cheese

2 (14- to 16-oz.) jars Alfredo sauce

9 lasagna noodles, cooked al dente

2 cups cooked chicken breast meat, diced

8 oz. low-fat shredded mozzarella cheese

8 oz. freshly shredded Parmesan cheese

❶ Heat oven to 350°F. Spray 13x9-inch pan with cooking spray.

❷ In medium bowl, stir together spinach, carrots, zucchini, onion, basil, oregano, nutmeg and garlic.

❸ In another medium bowl, stir egg substitute into the ricotta cheese, blending thoroughly.

Spread a thin layer of Alfredo sauce in bottom of prepared pan. Lay 3 noodles on top of sauce. Top with ½ of spinach mixture, ½ of ricotta cheese, 1 cup (more or less, to cover) Alfredo sauce and a generous sprinkle of mozzarella and Parmesan cheeses. Lay 3 more noodles on top and repeat layering of chicken and vegetables, sauce and cheeses. Top with last 3 noodles, remaining sauce and cheeses. Cover with aluminum foil, tenting it so the cheeses won't stick to it. Seal foil tightly around edge of pan. Bake 45 minutes. Uncover the last 5 minutes of baking. Let stand 10 minutes before serving.

❹ Variation: Use 2 cups (about 1 lb.) blanched shrimp. To blanch shrimp, shell and rinse in cool water. Bring 2 quarts of salted water to a rolling boil. Add shrimp and immediately remove pot from heat. Let shrimp stand in hot water one or two minutes; drain and put the shrimp into ice cold water to stop the cooking. When cool enough to handle, cut each shrimp into 3 or 4 pieces.

10 to 12 servings.

Chicken Lo Mein

CHICKEN LO MEIN

Ren & Vickie-Almony Evans, Baltimore, MD

3 tablespoons soy sauce

1 tablespoon dry sherry

2 tablespoons cornstarch

2 boneless skinless chicken breast halves, cut into ⅛-inch pieces

1 (8-oz.) pkg. linguine

¼ cup vegetable oil

½ lb. button mushrooms, sliced

¼ lb. Chinese pea pods

4 green onions, cut in 2-inch pieces

1 large red bell pepper, sliced ¼ inch thick

½ cup water

½ teaspoon chicken bouillon

1 In medium bowl, stir soy sauce, sherry and cornstarch; stir in chicken and set aside.

2 Cook linguine according to package directions; drain and keep warm.

3 In large skillet, heat oil over medium-high heat until hot. Add mushrooms, pea pods, onions and bell pepper; cook, stirring constantly, until crisp-tender, about 3 to 5 minutes. Remove with slotted spoon to medium bowl. Cook chicken mixture, stirring frequently, until chicken is no longer pink, about 3 minutes. Return vegetables to skillet along with water and chicken bouillon. Stir in linguine and continue cooking until heated through.

6 servings.

ZUCCHINI AND STEAK PIE

Corinne Earl, Boonville, NV

1 (15-oz.) box refrigerated pie crusts, 2 crusts

2½ cups zucchini or summer squash, cut into ½-inch-thick slices

2 small onions, sliced

1 tablespoon butter

Salt, to taste

Freshly ground pepper, to taste

Garlic powder, to taste

16-oz. cooked steak, cut into bite-size pieces

2 (10¾-oz.) cans cream of mushroom soup with garlic

5 oz. frozen spinach, cooked and squeezed

2 tablespoons Worcestershire sauce

1 Heat oven to 400°F. Place one pie crust in bottom of 9-inch pie plate.

2 Place squash and onions in large microwavable bowl. Microwave 3 minutes on high. Add butter to bowl and sprinkle with salt, pepper and garlic powder. Cook an additional 3 minutes or until tender.

3 Layer steak, 1 can soup, squash mixture, spinach and Worcestershire sauce and second can of soup into prepared crust. Cover with second crust and pinch edges together; cut slits in crust. Bake 45 minutes or until sauce is bubbling and crust is golden.

6 to 8 servings.

MEXICAN SURPRISE

Shirley Lee, San Francisco, CA

1 lb. ground beef

1 tablespoon minced onion

1/2 teaspoon garlic salt

2 (8-oz.) cans tomato sauce

3/4 cup chopped olives

1 cup sour cream

1 cup cottage cheese

1 (41/2-oz.) can chopped green chiles

1 (133/4-oz.) bag tortilla chips

2 cups shredded Monterey Jack cheese

❶ Heat oven to 350°F.

❷ Heat large skillet over medium heat. Add ground beef; cook until browned and drain. Stir in the onion, garlic salt, tomato sauce and olives; set aside.

❸ In medium bowl, stir together sour cream, cottage cheese and green chiles. Crush three-fourths of the tortilla chips and sprinkle over bottom of 13x9-inch baking dish. Spoon meat mixture over chips. Spoon cottage cheese mixture over beef. Sprinkle with cheese and top with remaining chips. Bake 30 to 35 minutes.

6 to 8 servings.

MOM'S FAMOUS CHICKEN AND DUMPLINGS

Henrietta Dinzler, Philadelphia, NY

1 whole chicken, cooked, bones and skin removed, cooking liquid reserved

Chicken bouillon, to taste

2 cups all-purpose flour

2 eggs

1/4 cup skim or 2% or whole milk

Frozen peas, carrots or broccoli, if desired

❶ Place chicken with its cooking liquid and bouillon in Dutch oven; bring to a boil.

❷ In large bowl, whisk flour, eggs and milk until combined. Drop flour mixture by teaspoonfuls into boiling chicken broth. Boil until dumplings float to the top. Add frozen vegetables. Thicken broth to gravy consistency, if necessary. Serve hot with bread, if desired.

4 to 6 servings.

TAMALE DISH

Crystal Organista, West Corvina, CA

1 lb. boneless skinless chicken breast halves

3 (12-oz.) cans tamales

2 (12-oz.) cans cream of broccoli soup

1 lb. shredded Monterey Jack cheese

❶ Heat oven to 350°F.

❷ Bring water to boil in large saucepan. Cook chicken in boiling water 20 minutes or until chicken is no longer pink in center; cool and shred.

❸ Meanwhile, place unwrapped tamales in 13x9-inch baking dish. Sprinkle tamales with shredded chicken; spread soup over chicken and sprinkle with cheese. Bake 35 to 45 minutes or until sauce is bubbling.

8 to 10 servings.

NON-STUFFED GREEN PEPPER CASSEROLE

Sandra Lee Eiselstein, Tipton, IA

3 cups (6 servings) minute rice, cooked

1½ lbs. ground beef

1 to 2 (14.5-oz.) cans diced tomatoes with basil, garlic, oregano

1 to 2 (8-oz.) cans tomato sauce

1 tablespoon butter

4 to 5 green peppers, chopped

1 (8-oz.) pkg. sliced button mushrooms

Garlic salt, to taste

2 to 3 cups shredded cheddar cheese

Soy sauce, to taste

1 Heat oven to 350°F. Spray 13x9-inch baking dish with cooking spray.

2 Spread rice in bottom of prepared baking dish.

3 In large skillet, brown beef over medium heat; drain. Stir in diced tomatoes and tomato sauce; simmer 10 minutes over low heat and spread evenly over rice. Melt butter in same skillet. Stir in peppers, mushrooms and garlic salt; cook until vegetables are tender. Spread over beef and sauce. Sprinkle with cheese. Bake until cheese melts. Serve with soy sauce.

8 servings.

ONE DISH CHICKEN CASSEROLE

Georgia Miller, Dover, NH

4 cups cubed herb seasoned stuffing

½ cup boiling water

1 tablespoon butter, melted

6 boneless skinless chicken breast halves

12 slices Swiss cheese

2 teaspoons smoked paprika

Salt, to taste

Freshly ground pepper, to taste

1 (10¾-oz.) can cream of chicken soup

⅓ cup milk

1 tablespoon chopped fresh parsley

1 Heat oven to 400°F.

2 In large bowl, stir together stuffing, water and butter; spread mixture onto bottom of 2- to 3-quart shallow baking dish. Top with chicken and sliced cheese. Sprinkle with paprika, salt and pepper.

3 In medium bowl, whisk together soup, milk and parsley. Pour mixture over chicken and stuffing. Bake, covered, 15 minutes. Uncover and bake an additional 15 minutes or until chicken is no longer pink.

6 servings.

PASTA SAUCE

Ann Stock, St Charles, MO

½ cup vegetable oil or bacon fat

3 slices bacon, cut into strips

2 lbs. ground beef or 1 lb. ground beef and 1 lb. ground pork

1 medium onion, diced

½ teaspoon garlic salt

½ teaspoon oregano

½ teaspoon basil

1 bay leaf

1 (28-oz.) can tomato sauce

1 (6-oz.) can tomato paste

1 In large skillet, heat oil over medium heat until hot. Add bacon; cook until crispy. Stir in ground beef, onion, garlic salt, oregano, basil and bay leaf and cook until beef is browned and onion is tender. Stir in tomato sauce and simmer over low heat 30 minutes. Stir in tomato paste and cook an additional 15 minutes; remove and discard bay leaf. Refrigerate overnight. Serve over pasta.

8 to 10 servings.

CHILI PIZZA

Enola R. Farrell, Union, MO

1 (13.8-oz.) refrigerated pizza crust

1 (14.3-oz.) can chili with or without beans

1 (10-oz.) pkg. chili cheese flavored corn chips, crushed

2 cups finely shredded cheese of choice

1 Heat oven to 350°F. Spray 13x9-inch baking pan with cooking spray.

2 Spread pizza crust across bottom and up sides of prepared pan. Bake crust according to package directions. Layer with chili, corn chips and cheese. Bake 15 to 20 minutes or until cheese melts and pizza crust is golden brown. Serve hot or cold.

6 to 8 servings.

POT PIES

Mable Watson, Lenoir, NC

1 (15-oz.) box refrigerated pie crust, 2 crusts

1 (10¾-oz.) can cream of potato soup

1 (10¾-oz.) can cream of chicken soup

1 (15-oz.) can mixed vegetables, drained

½ cup milk

½ teaspoon dried thyme

Freshly ground pepper, to taste

2 cups cooked, diced chicken or turkey

1 Heat oven to 375°F. Place one pie crust in 9-inch pie plate.

2 In large bowl, stir together potato soup, chicken soup, mixed vegetables, milk, thyme, pepper and chicken. Spoon mixture into prepared crust. Cover with remaining crust. Crimp edges to seal and slit top crust. Bake 40 minutes or until sauce is bubbling and crust is golden brown. Cool 10 minutes before serving.

6 to 8 servings.

CHEESY SPINACH CASSEROLE

Karin Schlenker, Powell, TN

1 (10-oz.) box frozen chopped spinach, cooked according to package directions, drained

½ lb. deli-style ham, cut into ¼-inch cubes

4 oz. shredded sharp cheddar cheese

1 (10¾-oz.) can low-fat cream of mushroom soup

1 tablespoon prepared mustard

4 hard-boiled eggs, chopped

1 Heat oven to 350°F.

2 Place spinach in 1½-quart baking dish. Stir in ham, cheese, mushroom soup and mustard. Sprinkle with egg. Bake 20 minutes or until heated through and cheese is melted.

3 to 4 servings.

QUICK CHICKEN STIR-FRY

Lisa Toedte, Centralia, IL

1 medium sweet onion, chopped

2 orange bell peppers, cut into thin strips

2 yellow bell peppers, cut into thin strips

3 portobello mushrooms, sliced

1 boneless skinless chicken breast half, cut into bite-size pieces

Salt, to taste

Freshly ground pepper, to taste

1 (10- to 16-oz.) bottle stir-fry sauce, to taste

1 Heat large, nonstick skillet over medium-high heat. Cook onion, bell peppers and mushrooms in skillet until softened and beginning to turn golden brown. Stir in chicken and continue cooking until chicken is no longer pink. Stir in salt, pepper and stir-fry sauce; cook until heated through. Serve over rice, if desired.

2 to 4 servings.

ITALIAN SHRIMP PASTA

Stephanie Massie, Mansfield, OH

½ cup butter

15 to 20 medium shelled, deveined uncooked shrimp

Freshly ground pepper, to taste

Italian seasoning, to taste

¼ teaspoon garlic salt

¼ teaspoon onion salt

Freshly grated Parmesan cheese

2 servings cooked linguine

1 In large skillet, melt butter over medium heat. Stir in shrimp and sprinkle with pepper, Italian seasoning, garlic salt and onion salt; cook 4 to 5 minutes or until shrimp turn pink. Sprinkle generously with Parmesan cheese and remove from skillet. Add linguine to butter sauce and cook until heated through. Serve shrimp over linguine with French bread dipped in the butter sauce, if desired.

2 servings.

SPAGHETTI CARBONARA

Maryellen Scheel, Hazelwood, MO

8 tablespoons butter

4 tablespoons olive oil

1 large onion, diced

1 lb. bacon, diced

1½ lbs. Italian sausage, cooked and diced

¾ cup dry white wine

2 lbs. spaghetti

5 eggs

6 oz. freshly grated Parmesan cheese, divided

1½ teaspoons granulated garlic

Salt, to taste

Freshly ground pepper, to taste

3 tablespoons chopped fresh parsley

1 In large skillet, melt butter and olive oil over medium heat, making sure butter does not burn. Add onion; cook until softened. Add bacon; cook until fat has rendered. Add sausage; cook until browned. Pour in white wine and increase heat to high; cook until wine is evaporated, then reduce heat to low.

2 Meanwhile, cook pasta according to package directions; drain, reserving 2 cups of cooking liquid, and pour into large bowl. Pour reserved cooking liquid into skillet.

3 In medium bowl, whisk eggs with 4 oz. of the cheese, garlic, salt and pepper. Pour hot meat mixture over spaghetti and stir in egg mixture; toss to combine. Sprinkle with remaining cheese and parsley.

4 servings.

SAUSAGE BAKE

Ann Stock, St Charles, MO

2 (5-oz.) boxes seasoned croutons

2 lbs. pork sausage, cooked and drained

2 cups shredded cheddar cheese

2 cups processed cheese spread loaf

2 (10¾-oz.) cans cream of mushroom soup

8 eggs

4 cups milk

1 Heat oven to 350°F. Spray 13x9-inch baking dish with cooking spray.

2 Sprinkle 1 box croutons over bottom of prepared dish; top with half the cooked sausage. Sprinkle with 1 cup of each cheese and add 1 can of soup. Repeat layers.

3 In medium bowl, whisk eggs and milk together; pour over casserole. Cover and refrigerate overnight. Bake, uncovered, 60 minutes or until heated through.

4 to 6 servings.

MAC AND CHEESE

Asia Vanatta, Alexandria, VA

1 (8-oz.) pkg. elbow macaroni

2 (8-oz.) pkgs. shredded cheddar cheese

1 (12-oz.) container small-curd cottage cheese

¼ cup freshly grated Parmesan cheese

1 (8-oz.) container sour cream

Salt, to taste

Freshly ground pepper, to taste

1 Heat oven to 350°F.

2 Cook pasta according to package directions; drain.

3 In 13x9-inch baking dish, stir together macaroni, cheeses, sour cream, salt and pepper. Bake 30 to 35 minutes or until bubbly and heated through.

4 to 6 servings.

NANCY'S SPAGHETTI GRAVY

Nancy Spark, Elk Grove, CA

3 lbs. lean ground beef

1 onion, chopped

4 garlic cloves, chopped

5 Italian sausages, cut into 1-inch pieces

2 cups dry porcini mushrooms, soaked in warm water, liquid reserved

2 to 3 tablespoons Italian seasoning

1 to 2 tablespoons dried oregano

1 to 2 tablespoons chopped fresh parsley

1 tablespoon crushed red pepper

Salt, to taste

Freshly ground pepper, to taste

1 (14½-oz.) can beef broth

½ cup sweet Marsala wine

1 (15-oz.) can tomato sauce or puree

1 (6-oz.) can tomato paste

1 tablespoon sugar

1 Heat large saucepan over medium-high heat. Add beef, onion and garlic; cook until meat is browned, stirring occasionally. Stir in sausage, mushrooms, Italian seasoning, oregano, parsley, crushed red pepper, salt and pepper; simmer 10 minutes. Stir in beef broth, Marsala wine, reserved mushroom liquid, tomato sauce, tomato paste and sugar; stir to combine. Bring to a boil, then simmer, covered, over low heat 1 hour. Serve with favorite pasta.

6 to 8 servings.

Nancy's Spaghetti Gravy

SUMMERTIME PASTA

Carla Siciliano, Munroe Falls, OH

3 tablespoons olive oil

3 garlic cloves, minced

1 large onion, diced

12 ripe Roma tomatoes, diced

1 (16-oz.) box farfalle pasta, cooked according to pkg. directions

8 oz. Fontana cheese, cubed

½ cup freshly shredded Parmesan cheese

½ cup fresh basil leaves, thinly sliced

Salt, to taste

Freshly ground pepper, to taste

1 In large skillet, heat oil over medium heat until hot. Add garlic; cook until fragrant, about 30 seconds to 1 minute. Add onion; cook until lightly browned. Stir in tomatoes, pasta, cheeses, basil, salt and pepper; cook until heated through. Serve with salad and crusty bread, if desired.

6 to 8 servings.

PASTA CON BROCCOLI

Ann Stock, St. Charles, MO

5 to 6 oz. shell shaped pasta

4 tablespoons butter

1 teaspoon minced garlic

1 cup broccoli florets

1 oz. sliced fresh mushrooms

2 cups cream or half-and-half

3 oz. freshly grated Parmesan cheese

1 oz. shredded provolone cheese

1 Cook pasta according to package directions; drain and return to same saucepan. Stir in butter, garlic, broccoli and mushrooms and cream; bring to a boil and remove from heat. Stir in cheeses. Serve warm.

4 servings.

TALLERINE

Joanna Gotlieb, Palm Beach Gardens, FL

2 tablespoons olive oil

1 medium onion, chopped

1 lb. ground beef

1 cup water

1 (15-oz.) can tomato sauce

2 (9-oz.) boxes medium egg noodles

1 (15-oz.) can corn

1 (7-oz.) can mushroom pieces

1 (5 to 6-oz.) can sliced black olives

Shredded sharp cheddar cheese

1 Heat oven to 350°F.

2 In large skillet, heat oil over medium heat. Add onion; cook until softened. Add beef; cook until brown. Stir in water, adding additional water if needed to moisten, tomato sauce and noodles. Cover and cook until noodles are tender. Stir in corn, mushrooms and olives. Pour into 2- to 3-quart baking dish. Bake 45 minutes. Sprinkle with cheese. Bake an additional 45 minutes. Let stand 15 minutes before serving.

6 to 8 servings.

TARRAGON CHICKEN CASSEROLE

Peggy M. Yamaguchi-Lazar, Eugene, OR

2 (10¾-oz.) cans low-fat condensed cream of chicken soup

2 cups evaporated skim milk

4 teaspoons dried tarragon

½ teaspoon freshly ground pepper

1 (16-oz.) pkg. linguine or spaghetti, cooked according to package directions; drained

6 cups cubed, cooked chicken breast

⅓ cup freshly grated Parmesan cheese

Paprika, if desired

1 Heat oven to 350°F.

2 In large bowl, stir together soup, evaporated milk, tarragon and black pepper. Stir in linguine and chicken. Pour into ungreased 4-quart baking dish. Sprinkle with Parmesan cheese and paprika. Bake, uncovered, 30 minutes or until heated through.

12 servings.

SHIPWRECK

Derrick Olsen, Modesto, CA

1 lb. ground beef, uncooked

1 onion, chopped

2 cups frozen tater tots

2 cups frozen mixed vegetables

1 (10¾-oz.) can cream of mushroom soup

¾ cup water

1 Heat oven to 375°F.

2 Layer uncooked hamburger, onion, tater tots, mixed vegetables and mushroom soup in 2- to 3-quart baking dish. Pour water around edges of dish. Bake 1 to 2 hours until beef is no longer pink and sauce is bubbling.

4 to 6 servings.

TURKEY OR CHICKEN STUFFING ROLL-UPS

Cynthia Sasek, Webb City, MO

1 (16-oz.) box turkey or chicken stuffing

1 lb. deli sliced turkey or chicken, about ⅛ inch thick

1 (12- to 16-oz.) jar or (1-oz.) pkg. turkey or chicken gravy

1 Heat oven to 350°F. Spray 13x9-inch baking dish with cooking spray.

2 Cook stuffing according to package directions. Spoon stuffing onto one end of meat, spreading the entire width of the meat; roll meat up around stuffing jelly-roll style. Place in prepared dish.

3 If using dry gravy mix, prepare according to directions. Pour gravy over rolls. Cover dish with aluminum foil and bake 20 minutes. Remove foil and bake an additional 5 to 10 minutes.

4 to 6 servings.

LIGHTER FETTUCCINE ALFREDO

Stacia Chivilo, Indian Head Park, IL

1 cup butter

2 cups non-fat or light ricotta cheese

1 cup freshly grated Romano or Parmesan cheese

1 cup milk

Freshly ground pepper, to taste

Garlic powder, to taste

Chopped fresh parsley, to taste

1 lb. fettuccine, cooked

1 In medium saucepan, melt butter over medium-low heat. Add ricotta cheese, Romano cheese, milk, pepper, garlic powder and parsley; cook until heated through and sauce has thickened, stirring often. Stir in fettuccine.

4 to 6 servings.

VEGETARIAN ENCHILADAS

Melodee Seal, Tampa, FL

2 cups mashed potatoes

8 oz. container sour cream

½ cup chopped onion

2 teaspoons minced garlic

Shredded cheese of choice

Bacon, if desired

Lettuce, if desired

Tomatoes, if desired

12 (8- to 9-inch) flour tortillas for burritos

1 (10-oz.) can enchilada sauce

1 Heat oven to 350°F.

2 In large bowl, combine potatoes, sour cream, onion, garlic and some of the cheese. Stir in bacon, lettuce and tomatoes, if desired. Fill tortillas with potato mixture; roll up and place in 13x9-inch baking dish. Pour enchilada sauce over rolls and sprinkle with remaining cheese. Bake 15 to 20 minutes or until heated through.

6 to 8 servings.

RING CASSEROLE

Jayne Leight, Stacy, MN

1 (7-oz.) box small ring pasta

1 (10¾-oz.) can cream of chicken soup

¼ cup milk

1 (5-oz.) can Hormel lean ham, chopped

1 Heat oven to 325°F.

2 Cook pasta according to package directions; drain.

3 In large bowl, stir together pasta, soup, milk and ham. Pour into ungreased 2- to 3-quart baking dish. Bake 1 hour or until bubbling. Serve with French bread, if desired.

2 to 4 servings.

WHITE CHILI

Ginger Pierce, Madison, AL

6 cups water

5 chicken bouillon cubes

8 boneless chicken breast halves

5 tablespoons olive oil

1 large onion, chopped

3 tablespoons minced garlic

1 (10¾-oz.) can cream of chicken soup

2 (14-oz.) cans Northern beans

2 (14-oz.) cans white whole kernel corn

2 (4½-oz.) cans chopped green chiles

3 tablespoons chili powder

1 tablespoon white pepper

1 tablespoon dried oregano

2 teaspoons ground cumin

2 tablespoons Louisiana hot sauce

4 cups shredded Monterey Jack cheese

1 small container sour cream, if desired

1 (13¾-oz.) bag tortilla chips, if desired

1 In large saucepan, bring water and bouillon cubes to a boil. Add chicken; boil until chicken is no longer pink in center. Remove chicken from broth; cool and shred. Reserve 5 cups of broth.

2 In large skillet, heat oil over medium heat until hot. Add onion and garlic; cook until tender.

3 In large saucepan, stir together 3 cups of the broth, onions, chicken, soup, beans, corn, chiles, chili powder, white pepper, oregano, cumin and hot sauce; bring to a boil. Lower temperature and simmer 1 hour, adding additional reserved broth if chili seems too thick. Add 3 cups Monterey Jack cheese and stir until melted. Serve topped with remaining cheese and sour cream. Serve with crackers or cornbread, if desired.

4 To serve cold, store in refrigerator overnight or at least 4 hours. Serve over tortilla chips or crackers. Garnish with jalapeño peppers, if desired.

6 to 8 servings.

BAKED JUMBO SHRIMP

Marge Laughlin, Pembroke Pines, FL

STUFFING

8 tablespoons butter

2 tablespoons minced shallot

3 ribs celery, diced

½ lb. baby shrimp, whole

½ lb. white fish, cubed

½ lb. scallops, halved

1½ cups dried bread crumbs

Salt, to taste

Freshly ground black pepper, to taste

1 teaspoon paprika

1 teaspoon dried thyme

⅛ teaspoon cayenne pepper

2 tablespoons dry sherry

¼ cup chopped fresh parsley

1 egg, beaten

SAUCE

8 tablespoons butter, divided

2 tablespoons chopped shallots

¼ cup Chablis or other white wine

1 cup heavy cream

Dash cayenne pepper

Salt, to taste

Freshly ground pepper, to taste

SHRIMP

20 shelled, deveined uncooked extra-large shrimp

4 tablespoons butter, melted

3 tablespoons white wine

Paprika, to taste

1 For Stuffing: Melt butter in large skillet and cook shallots and celery over medium heat until tender, about 5 minutes. Add seafood and cook 2 minutes until cooked through. Add bread crumbs and seasonings and stir to combine. Stir in sherry and parsley; remove from heat; cool slightly and stir in egg.

2 For Sauce: Heat 2 tablespoons butter in small skillet and cook shallots over medium heat until soft, about 3 to 5 minutes. Add wine and cook over medium heat until reduced, about 5 to 10 minutes. Stir in cream and reduce until thickened, about 6 to 8 minutes. Season with cayenne, salt and pepper; remove from heat and stir in remaining butter until melted.

3 For Shrimp: Heat oven to 350°F. Butter large, shallow baking dish large enough to hold shrimp in a single layer. Place 2 tablespoons stuffing into the cavity of each shrimp and arrange in prepared dish. Pour melted butter and white wine over and sprinkle with paprika. Bake 15 to 20 minutes until the shrimp are pink and cooked through. To serve, place some cooked rice on each plate and arrange shrimp over rice; cover with the white wine sauce.

6 to 8 servings.

WARM SEASONED CREAM CHEESE WRAPPED IN GRAPE LEAVES

Beth Bangert, Delano, MN

2 to 3 large garlic cloves

Extra-virgin olive oil

Sea salt, to taste

1 loaf baguette bread, sliced

1 jar grape leaves in brine, drained, liquid reserved

2 (8-oz.) pkgs. cream cheese

1/8 teaspoon seasoned salt

Dash ground chipotle pepper

4 to 5 sun-dried tomato halves, softened and finely diced, if desired

2 sun-dried red bell peppers, softened and finely diced

2 fresh basil leaves, chopped

1 Heat oven to 375°F.

2 Coat garlic cloves with olive oil and sprinkle with sea salt. Brush each slice of baguette with olive oil and place on baking sheet along with garlic and bake until lightly toasted.

3 Separate grape leaves; rinse 5 to 6 leaves and blot dry. Trim stems and lay leaves on work surface to form a bed for cheese ball. Leave remaining leaves in brine.

4 Stir together cheese, roasted garlic, salt and chipotle pepper in large bowl until combined; form into a ball and flatten. Coat with olive oil and press one side into sun-dried tomatoes. Press other side into the sun-dried red bell peppers. Place in the center of the grape leaves and pull the leaves up and over to completely encase cheese. Patch any holes with additional leaves if necessary.

5 Place cheese ball onto a square of aluminum foil and brush with olive oil to coat. Pull up sides of foil over cheese and pinch corners to seal. Bake 20 minutes or until warmed through. Serve with the baguette slices. If desired, cheese can be refrigerated before baking up to 3 days ahead.

12 servings.

ROASTED SWEET POTATO ROUNDS

Nancy F. McCune, San Diego, CA

3 lbs. sweet potatoes, peeled and sliced into 3/4-inch slices

Olive oil

Salt, to taste

Freshly ground pepper, to taste

Sour cream

Chopped fresh chives

1 Heat oven to 375°F.

2 Place sweet potato in large roasting pan and toss with olive oil to coat. Sprinkle with salt and pepper; roast 1 hour, turning once.

3 To serve, top with a dollop of sour cream and chives. Pass on tray lined with one piece of banana leaf. Rounds can be cooked in advance and reheated 15 minutes before serving, if desired.

24 servings.

EGGNOG-SWEET POTATO CASSEROLE

Linda McCall, North Richland Hills, TX

4 cups canned sweet potatoes from 2 (17.2-oz. cans)

2 tablespoons melted butter

1 cup eggnog

Salt, to taste

6 pineapple slices

2 tablespoons packed brown sugar

1 Heat oven to 375°F. Cook sweet potatoes as directed on can. Whip sweet potatoes in large bowl until smooth and fluffy. Add butter, eggnog and salt. Beat until thoroughly combined. Spoon into 3-quart baking dish. Top with pineapple slices and sprinkle with brown sugar. Bake 25 to 30 minutes or until heated through.

6 to 8 servings.

RUMAKI

Clare Morgan-Heupel, Duluth, MN

1 cup soy sauce

¼ cup dry sherry

2 tablespoons coarsely chopped fresh ginger

3 garlic cloves, coarsely chopped or sliced

24 pieces chicken livers

12 slices bacon, halved lengthwise

1 (4-oz.) can sliced water chestnuts, drained

1 Heat oven to 375°F.

2 In large, resealable plastic bag, combine soy sauce, sherry, ginger and garlic. Add chicken livers; toss to coat. Refrigerate 2 to 4 hours.

3 Place bacon on baking sheet and bake until half done; drain on paper towels. Remove livers from marinade and pat dry; discard marinade.

4 Place 1 chicken liver piece on each bacon half and top with water chestnut slice. Roll up and secure with a toothpick. Place rumaki on baking sheet; increase oven to 450°F and bake until bacon is cooked through but not crispy and chicken liver is cooked through. Serve hot.

10 to 12 servings.

GORGONZOLA YAMS

Jean Potter, Long Beach, CA

4 yams or sweet potatoes, peeled and thinly sliced

Seasoned olive oil or extra-virgin olive oil

1 cup crumbled Gorgonzola cheese

½ cup finely chopped walnuts

1 Heat oven to 350°F.

2 Layer yams in 13x9-inch baking dish; drizzle with oil. Bake 40 minutes, or until tender when pierced with a fork. Remove from oven and sprinkle with cheese and walnuts. Bake an additional 10 minutes or until cheese is just melted.

4 to 6 servings.

CHOCOLATE OBLIVION TORTE WITH RASPBERRY SAUCE

Maryellen Scheel, Hazelwood, MO

TORTE

1 lb. semisweet chocolate

8 oz. butter

4 eggs

RASPBERRY SAUCE

1½ lbs. raspberries

Sugar, to taste

1 For Torte: Heat oven to 375°F. Cut a piece of parchment paper into a circle to fit the bottom of a 10-inch springform pan. Butter parchment paper and spray pan with cooking spray. Over hot (not boiling) water in medium saucepan, melt chocolate and butter together in a medium stainless bowl. In large bowl over simmering water, heat eggs, stirring constantly; cook until just warm to touch. Remove from heat and beat until triple in volume and soft peaks form. Incorporate chocolate mixture into eggs and fold until just blended. Place springform pan in large pan at least 2 inches deep. Pour chocolate mixture into prepared pan. Pour 1 inch of very hot water around springform pan. Bake 5 minutes. Cover loosely with buttered foil and bake an additional 10 minutes. Cool 45 minutes. Cover and chill overnight. Remove cake from springform pan wiping bottom of pan with hot, damp towel to release torte. Place cake round on top and invert.

2 For Sauce: Puree raspberries and sugar in blender. Bring to a boil in medium saucepan and let simmer until thickened to desired consistency. To serve, place raspberry sauce on plate and top with torte; drizzle with additional raspberry sauce.

14 servings.

Chocolate Oblivion Torte with Raspberry Sauce

RED PEPPER CREAM SAUCE WITH TORTELLINI

Cathy Bush, Virginia Beach, VA

1 tablespoon butter

1 teaspoon olive oil

2 large red bell peppers, chopped

3 carrots, chopped

1 large onion, chopped

3 garlic cloves, minced

1 tablespoon mixed crushed peppercorns

1 cup milk, divided

1 tablespoon cornstarch

Salt, to taste

White pepper, to taste

2 (9-oz.) pkgs. fresh tortellini or other pasta

1 Melt butter and olive oil in large saucepan and cook bell peppers, carrots and onion until softened. Stir in garlic and peppercorns; cook 1 minute until fragrant.

2 Pour vegetables into blender and puree until smooth. Return pureed vegetables back to saucepan with ½ cup milk; bring to a simmer and stir in remaining milk blended with cornstarch. Continue to cook until mixture comes to a boil and thickens, stirring frequently. Stir in salt and pepper.

3 Prepare tortellini according to package directions; toss with sauce and serve immediately with crusty French bread, if desired. If desired stir cooked peas and mushrooms into sauce.

4 to 6 servings.

HOLIDAY BREAD

Kathy Allred, Tucson, AZ

⅓ cup Crisco

1 cup packed brown sugar

2 eggs

For banana or banana nut bread, 1 cup banana and 1 cup chopped walnuts, if desired

For pumpkin or applesauce bread, 1 cup canned pumpkin or applesauce, ½ cup raisins, and ½ cup chopped walnuts

¼ cup milk

2 tablespoons water (if using butter, omit water)

2 cups all-purpose flour

2 teaspoons baking powder

½ teaspoon salt

¼ teaspoon baking soda

Raisins, if desired

Nuts, if desired

1 teaspoon ground cinnamon

½ teaspoon ground nutmeg

1 Heat oven to 350°F.

2 Cream together shortening and sugar in large bowl. Add eggs and combine well. Stir in banana, pumpkin or applesauce for type of bread desired. Stir in milk and water until combined. Add flour, baking powder, salt and baking soda, a little at a time, until combined. Add walnuts and raisins, if desired. Bake in lightly greased pans, 60 to 65 minutes for large loaves or 30 to 35 minutes for smaller loaves until toothpick inserted in center comes out clean. Cool in pan 10 to 15 minutes. Remove from pan and cool completely before slicing.

12 to 16 servings.

CHOCOLATE DREAM CAKE

Linda Galyean, El Dorado Hills, CA

CAKE

1 (18¼-oz.) devil's food cake mix

1 cup sour cream

1 cup water

⅓ cup vegetable oil

3 eggs

FROSTING

7 oz. bittersweet chocolate, chopped

2½ cups heavy cream, chilled, divided

4 tablespoons light corn syrup

1 tablespoon vanilla extract

4 egg yolks

5 tablespoons instant vanilla pudding mix

GLAZE

½ cup heavy whipping cream

1 tablespoon light corn syrup

4 oz. bittersweet or semisweet chocolate, chopped

2 oz. dark chocolate, chopped

1 tablespoon unsalted butter, room temperature

GARNISH

Whipped cream or whipped white frosting

❶ For Cake: Heat oven to 350°F. Lightly grease and flour two 9-inch cake pans. In large bowl, combine cake mix, sour cream, water, vegetable oil and eggs; beat at high speed 2 minutes, scraping sides of bowl as needed. Pour into prepared pans. Bake 25 to 35 minutes, or until toothpick inserted in center comes out clean. Cool cakes in pans on wire racks 15 minutes. Remove from pans and cool completely.

❷ For Frosting: Microwave chocolate on high 90 seconds until melted, stirring at 30-second intervals; set aside to cool. In small, heavy saucepan over medium-low heat, whisk together ½ cup cream, corn syrup, vanilla and egg yolks. Cook, whisking constantly, 5 to 6 minutes or until mixture is thickened and coats back of spoon and reaches 160°F on instant-read thermometer. Do not overcook. Strain yolk mixture into chocolate. Whisk briskly, until chocolate is shiny and smooth. Cool to 85°F. In large bowl, beat remaining 2 cups cream and vanilla pudding at medium-high speed until stiff peaks form; fold cooled chocolate mixture into whipped cream. To frost cake, lay first layer flat-side up; generously frost leaving a thick layer of frosting in center. Top with last cake layer, flat-side down, pressing slightly, and frost with remaining frosting; refrigerate 1 hour

❸ For Glaze: Bring cream and corn syrup to simmer in small saucepan. Remove from heat. Add chocolates; let stand 5 minutes. Stir until smooth. Add butter; stir until melted. Let stand until lukewarm but still pourable, about 20 minutes. Pour evenly over frosting and refrigerate. Garnish with whipped cream or whipped white frosting.

10 to 12 servings.

MOLTEN CHOCOLATE CAKES

Maryellen Scheel, Hazelwood, MO

CAKE

12 oz. melted unsalted butter

12 oz. semisweet chocolate chips

7½ large eggs

6 oz. sugar

Dash salt

2 tablespoons all-purpose flour

12 extra-large paper muffin cups

GARNISH

4 oz. powdered sugar

4 oz. chocolate syrup

1 Heat oven to 425°F.

2 Melt butter and chocolate in medium heatproof bowl over medium saucepan of simmering water; remove from heat. Beat eggs, sugar and salt with whisk in medium bowl until sugar dissolves. Beat egg mixture into chocolate until smooth. Add flour until just combined.

3 Line muffin pans with papers and spray papers with cooking spray. Divide batter evenly into muffin cups. Bake 8 to 10 minutes; center will not be set. Remove cakes to serving platter. Remove paper liners and sprinkle cakes with powdered sugar and drizzle with chocolate syrup. Serve immediately.

12 servings.

SPIEDIS

John M. Baker, Twentynine Palms, CA

1 5- to 7-lb. leg of lamb, de-boned, trimmed

1 tablespoon kosher (coarse) salt

1 tablespoon freshly ground pepper

4 tablespoons chopped fresh or 2 tablespoons dried rosemary

4 tablespoons chopped fresh or 2 tablespoons dried mint

3 garlic cloves, minced

1 medium yellow onion, minced

2 tablespoons extra- virgin olive oil

Juice of 1 lemon

1 Cut lamb into 1½-inch pieces and place lamb in a large, resealable plastic bag.

2 In large bowl, stir together salt, pepper, rosemary, mint, garlic, onion, olive oil and lemon juice; pour over lamb and seal bag. Refrigerate overnight.

3 Remove lamb from marinade; discard marinade. Heat grill. Place lamb on skewers and cook on gas grill over medium-high heat or on charcoal grill 4 to 6 inches from medium-hot coals. Cook until medium rare, about 8 to 12 minutes.

12 to 16 servings.

STANDING RIB ROAST

Vickie Williams, Gary, IN

4- to 6-lb. prime rib roast

1 to 2 garlic cloves, thinly sliced

Extra-virgin olive oil, to taste

Freshly ground pepper

Ground mustard, to taste

1 Heat oven to 325°F. Using small, sharp knife, make slits over the top of the roast. Insert garlic slices into each slit. Rub the roast with oil, ground pepper and mustard. Bake 25 to 35 minutes per pound, depending on your preference, shorter time for rare, longer time for well-done. Cover loosely with aluminum foil and let rest 10 to 15 minutes before slicing.

4 to 6 servings.

TIRAMISÚ

John Dineen, Wauwatosa, WI

CAKE

8 eggs, room temperature, separated

2 cups sugar

2 teaspoons white vinegar

2 cups all-purpose flour, sifted before measuring

SOAKING LIQUID

1½ cups strong coffee

½ cup crème de cacao or another liqueur

CHEESE FILLING

6 eggs, separated

⅔ cup sugar

24 oz. mascarpone cheese, softened

8 oz. bittersweet chocolate, coarsely chopped

TOPPING

1 pint whipping cream

¼ cup sugar

1 teaspoon unsweetened cocoa

1 For Cake: Heat oven to 350°F. Beat egg whites in large bowl until fluffy; slowly beat in sugar. In separate, large bowl stir together egg yolks and vinegar and beat into whites. Slowly beat flour into egg mixture. Pour half of the batter into two ungreased pans that will be used for serving. Pour the other half of batter into 14x18x1-inch baking pan lined with waxed paper. Bake 12 to 15 minutes until a toothpick inserted in center comes out clean. Cool, if possible, upside down so the sponge cake does not shrink.

2 For Soaking Liquid: Stir together coffee and liqueur in medium bowl; pour half of the mixture over reserved, uncooked batter.

3 For Cheese Filling: Beat egg whites in large bowl until fluffy. Whisk egg yolks and sugar over double boiler. Mix in the egg whites and stir in softened mascarpone cheese. Fold the chocolate into the egg mixture. Spread the cheese mixture over the soaked sponge cake.

4 For Topping: Remove waxed paper from other sponge cake carefully so that it fits over the cheese mixture in the two pans. Pour the remaining coffee/liqueur mixture over the cakes so that it soaks in. Whip the cream and sugar and, using a rubber spatula, spread over the two cakes covering any cracks in the sponge cake and also keeping in the moisture. Sprinkle the cocoa over the cakes for decoration. Let sit, covered and refrigerated for at least 24 hours before serving. Refrigerate leftovers.

10 to 12 servings.

Summer White Sangria

SUMMER WHITE SANGRIA

Lissa Carrino, Medina, OH

¾ cup sugar

1½ cups apricot brandy

2 fresh apricots, chopped

2 fresh plums, chopped

2 fresh peaches, chopped

20 grapes, halved

2 bottles Sauvignon Blanc

Lemon-lime flavored carbonated soda

Lime slices

1 In large pitcher, stir together sugar and brandy. Stir in fruits. Refrigerate 4 to 12 hours. Thirty minutes prior to serving, add wine. Stir and return to refrigerator. To serve, pour wine mixture with fruit into tall serving glasses three-fourths full. Top with lemon-lime soda and garnish with lime slices.

12 to 24 servings.

BACKYARD BBQ POTATO SALAD

Mary Arredondo, Billings, MT

6 medium russet potatoes, unpeeled

1 cup chopped celery

½ cup chopped onions

⅓ cup bread-and-butter cucumber chips

2 teaspoons sugar

2 teaspoons celery seed

2 teaspoons vinegar

2 teaspoons prepared mustard

1½ teaspoons salt

1¼ cups salad dressing

3 hard-boiled eggs, chopped

1 Boil whole potatoes in large saucepan of salted water 40 minutes or until tender; drain. Peel and cube; place in large bowl. In medium bowl, combine celery, onions, cucumber, sugar, celery seed, vinegar, mustard and salt. Add salad dressing and mix into potatoes. Fold in chopped eggs. Cover and chill.

10 to 12 servings.

WHITE RUSSIAN CHOCOLATE FUDGE POUND CAKE

Stas' Trakul, Denver, CO

1 (18¼-oz.) pkg. chocolate cake mix

1 (4-serving size) pkg. instant chocolate pudding

¼ cup vegetable oil

4 eggs

½ cup vodka

¾ cup coffee flavored liqueur

½ cup half-and-half

1 (8-oz.) container frozen whipped topping, thawed

1 (10-oz.) jar maraschino cherries with stems, drained

1 Heat oven to 350°F. Grease and flour 12-cup Bundt pan.

2 Stir together cake mix, pudding, oil, eggs, vodka, coffee liqueur and half-and-half in large bowl; beat at medium speed 2 minutes. Pour batter into prepared pan and bake 55 minutes or until a toothpick inserted in center comes out clean; cool completely.

3 Using a serrated knife, mark off ½-inch intervals on top of cake all the way around and ½- to 1-inch-deep cuts to make a well in the cake. Remove cut pieces.

4 Place whipped topping in pastry bag with decorative tip and pipe the whipped cream into the well of the cake even with the top. Switch tips to a large star tip and evenly pipe stars on top of the cream in the well. Top with cherries. Store in refrigerator.

10 to 12 servings.

LINGUINE WITH WHITE SEAFOOD SAUCE

Michele Armstrong, Gardnerville, NV

PASTA

1-lb. pkg. fettuccine or linguine noodles

1 tablespoon butter

SAUCE

2 tablespoons olive oil

3 garlic cloves, minced

2-oz. bottled clam juice

2 (10½-oz.) cans white clam sauce with garlic and herbs

½ teaspoon crushed red pepper

1 (6½-oz.) can chopped clams, drained

1 (10-oz.) can whole baby clams

¼ lb. clams in shell

1 (6½-oz.) can lump crabmeat

¼ lb. baby scallops

¼ lb. shelled, deveined uncooked large shrimp

¼ lb. baby cooked shrimp

½ cup Chardonnay

¼ cup chopped fresh parsley

¼ cup chopped fresh basil

2 teaspoons fresh lemon juice

¼ cup creamy Alfredo sauce

1 Prepare linguine according to package directions; drain. Add butter to pasta and keep warm.

2 In large skillet, heat oil over medium heat until hot. Add garlic; cook 30 seconds to 1 minute or until fragrant. Stir in clam juice, clam sauce and red pepper; bring to a boil, reduce heat, and simmer 5 minutes. Stir in chopped clams, whole baby clams, clams in shell, lump crabmeat, scallops, shrimp, cooked shrimp, Chardonnay, parsley, basil, lemon juice and Alfredo sauce; bring to a boil, then simmer 3 minutes or until scallops and shrimp turn pink and clam shells have opened. To serve, toss sauce with pasta.

8 servings.

MINI LAMB CHOPS WITH ARTICHOKE DIP

Brian Redman, Louisville, KY

Olive oil, to taste

16 baby lamb chops

Salt, to taste

Freshly ground pepper, to taste

1 can artichoke hearts, drained

1 jar marinated mushrooms, undrained

1 shallot, chopped

4 sprigs fresh tarragon

Olive oil, to taste

1 Heat grill.

2 Drizzle olive oil over both sides of chops and sprinkle with salt and pepper. Grill chops on gas grill over medium heat or on charcoal grill 4 to 6 inches from medium coals; cover grill. Cook lamb to desired doneness.

3 Meanwhile, place artichoke hearts, mushrooms, shallot and tarragon in food processor; pulse to coarsely chop and drizzle in olive oil to desired thickness. Place chops on serving platter and serve with the artichoke dip.

16 servings.

HOUSEHOLD FRAGRANCE

Mable Watson, Lenoir, NC

2 cinnamon sticks

Peel from 2 lemons, 2 oranges and 1 grapefruit

1 tablespoon whole cloves

1 tablespoon ground allspice

Medium saucepan of water

1 Pour cinnamon sticks, peel, cloves, allspice and water into saucepan; bring to a boil. Reduce heat and simmer on low to give your house a festive air. Do not drink. Discard when done.

LINDA'S GUMBO

Linda Hart, Tempe, AZ

10 cups water

2 teaspoons sea salt

1 garlic clove

Celery rib, chopped

1 green bell pepper, quartered

1 onion, quartered

2 lbs. medium shelled, deveined uncooked shrimp, shells saved for stock

1 tablespoon chopped fresh parsley

1 teaspoon freshly ground black pepper

1 teaspoon cayenne pepper

1 tablespoon Cajun seasoning

1 tablespoon gumbo filé powder

Salt, to taste

12 tablespoons butter, melted

1 large white onion, chopped

1 bunch green onions, sliced

$\frac{1}{2}$ bell pepper, chopped

$\frac{1}{2}$ cup celery, chopped

$1\frac{1}{2}$ cups okra, sliced or 10-oz. pkg. frozen okra, thawed, if desired

1 lb. Andouille sausage or spicy smoked sausage, cut into small pieces

1 lb. boneless skinless chicken breast halves or thighs, cut into small pieces

$\frac{1}{2}$ cup flour

4 cups hot cooked rice

1 Place water, salt, garlic, vegetables, and shrimp shells in large saucepan; bring to a boil and simmer 30 minutes or until stock has reduced by half. Strain out shells and vegetables; place stock back in saucepan over medium heat and stir in parsley, black pepper, cayenne pepper, Cajun seasoning, gumbo filé and salt.

2 In large, heavy skillet cook 4 tablespoons butter and vegetables over medium heat until crisp-tender. Stir in sausage, chicken and shrimp and continue cooking until chicken is no longer pink in center. Remove from heat.

3 Add remaining butter to large saucepan or Dutch oven; whisk in flour and cook 4 to 5 minutes or until roux has a nutty aroma and is beginning to turn light golden brown. Whisk in stock and cook, stirring frequently until thickened. Stir in cooked vegetables and meat. To serve, place $\frac{1}{2}$ cup cooked rice in large soup bowls and ladle gumbo over.

6 to 8 servings.

APPLE CALVADOS CREAM SAUCE WITH PORK

Jodi Paige Walker, Tucson, AZ

PORK

1 lb. pork tenderloin or 3 boneless pork chops

4 tablespoons butter, divided

4 medium golden delicious apples, peeled, sliced ¼ inch thick

1 tablespoon sugar

SAUCE

1 tablespoon butter

2 large shallots, minced

1 tablespoon chopped fresh thyme or 1 teaspoon dried thyme

⅓ cup Calvados or apple brandy

⅓ cup apple cider

1 cup whipping cream

Salt, to taste

Freshly ground pepper, to taste

1 For Pork: Pound pork slices into ¼-inch-thick medallions, using meat mallet. Melt 2 tablespoons of the butter in large skillet over medium heat. Add apple slices and sugar; cook on both sides until golden brown; remove and keep warm. Melt remaining 2 tablespoons butter in same skillet over medium-high heat and cook pork until cooked through, about 2 minutes per side; transfer to serving platter.

2 For Sauce: Melt 1 tablespoon butter in same skillet over medium heat. Add shallots and thyme; sauté 2 minutes. Add Calvados and boil until reduced to a glaze, scraping up any brown bits. Stir in apple cider and cream; simmer until mixture thickens to sauce consistency, about 3 minutes. Season with salt and pepper. To serve, arrange a few pork medallions on each plate. Spoon sauce over meat; top with apples.

4 servings.

PORK LOIN WITH PEACH SAUCE

Karin B. Schlenker, Powell, TN

1 lb. pork loin

Salt, to taste

Freshly ground pepper, to taste

½ cup packed brown sugar

¼ cup Worcestershire sauce

1 tablespoon mulling spices or hot apple cider drink mix

2 large peaches, peeled and finely diced

1 Heat oven to 350°F.

2 Place pork loin in small roasting pan and sprinkle with salt and pepper.

3 Combine brown sugar, Worcestershire sauce, mulling spices and peaches in small bowl and spoon over pork. Cook pork, basting with sauce every 10 minutes, until meat thermometer inserted in thickest part reaches 145°, approximately 40 minutes.

4 To serve, slice into 1-inch-thick slices and top with peach sauce. Serve over rice or cooked millet, if desired.

3 to 4 servings.

Pork Loin with Peach Sauce

CILANTRO SALMON SALAD

Debbie Ellis, Moreno Valley, CA

5 cups chopped fresh cilantro leaves

8 garlic cloves, minced

1 small jalapeño, minced

1 habanero chile, chopped

1 cup chopped red onion

¼ cup chopped green pepper

¼ cup chopped red pepper

5 green onions, sliced

1 (6-oz.) can black olives, chopped

1 tablespoon crushed red pepper

1 tablespoon dried oregano

1½ lbs. firm tomatoes, chopped

1 (4-oz.) can chopped green chiles

¾ cup sugar

½ cup fresh lemon juice

1½ tablespoons vinegar

1 lb. salmon fillet

¼ cup fresh lime juice

¼ teaspoon salt

¼ teaspoon freshly ground black pepper

Tortilla chips, coarsely crushed

1 Heat oven to broil.

2 In large bowl, stir together cilantro, garlic, jalapeño and habanero chiles, chopped red onion, green pepper, red pepper, green onions, chopped olives, red pepper, oregano, tomatoes, chopped green chiles and sugar; mix well.

3 In small bowl, combine the lemon juice and vinegar. Pour over salad and stir to combine. Refrigerate.

4 Place salmon on aluminum-foil-lined baking sheet. Broil 5 minutes; turn over and broil an additional 5 minutes until salmon flakes easily with a fork. Transfer to cutting board. Pour lime juice over salmon and break into small pieces with fork. Fold salmon, salt and pepper gently into salad.

5 Divide salad evenly among six plates. Sprinkle with crushed tortillas; serve immediately.

6 servings.

CRAB AND CUCUMBER ROLLS

Johnnie Hawkes, Bedford, VA

1 large cucumber

1 (6½-oz.) can crabmeat

4 tablespoons mayonnaise

1½ teaspoons finely grated onion

Dash salt

½ teaspoon sugar

5 dashes hot pepper sauce

1 Slice off ends of cucumber and cut into 3 equal pieces. Remove seeds, making a large cavity.

2 In medium bowl, stir together crabmeat, mayonnaise, onion, salt, sugar and hot pepper sauce. Stuff crab mixture into cucumber cavity.

3 Wrap cucumber with plastic wrap and refrigerate until chilled. Slice into ½-inch-thick slices to serve.

12 servings.

LEG OF LAMB

Jo Oliver, Leesburg, FL

1 5-lb. leg of lamb

1 head of fresh garlic, separated, peeled, cloves halved

1 tablespoon fresh rosemary

1 Heat oven to 350°F.

2 Pierce skin of meat in several places making slits for garlic and rosemary. Place one piece garlic and some rosemary into each slit. Bake 30 to 35 minutes per pound of meat. Remove meat from pan; let rest 5 minutes and cut into slices; cover loosely with aluminum foil.

3 Meanwhile, deglaze pan by adding water from cooking vegetables (string beans and potatoes) or beef broth. Mix 2 tablespoons flour in a small amount of water and pour into pan stirring constantly. Cook until gravy comes to a boil; strain. If desired, place in a degreasing pitcher to remove excess fat.

12 to 16 servings.

EGGPLANT "CAVIAR" (PÂTE)

Dzhangirova Sveteana, Seattle, WA

1 large eggplant (about 1 lb.), finely chopped

3 tablespoons plus 1 teaspoon salt, divided

3 tablespoons vegetable or olive oil, divided

⅔ cup chopped onion

1 (8-oz.) can whole plum tomatoes, undrained

3 garlic cloves, minced

1 red bell pepper, finely chopped

¼ teaspoon freshly ground pepper

5 tablespoons finely chopped fresh herbs, such as cilantro, parsley and basil

1 In large bowl, cover eggplant and 3 tablespoons salt with water; let stand 15 to 20 minutes. Rinse and drain.

2 In large skillet, heat 2 tablespoons oil over medium-high heat until hot. Add onion; cook until softened and lightly browned. Stir in tomatoes with their juice; cover and cook, stirring occasionally, about 8 minutes. Add garlic and bell pepper; cook an additional 3 to 5 minutes. Remove from heat.

3 In separate large skillet, heat remaining oil over medium-high heat. Add eggplant; cook 10 minutes, stirring occasionally. Stir tomato mixture into eggplant; reduce heat and simmer, uncovered, 5 minutes. Season with remaining salt, pepper and herbs. Serve warm or cold.

6 to 8 servings.

CAJUN FRIED CHICKEN BREAST

Craig Morgan, Salisbury, MD

CHICKEN

4 boneless chicken breast halves

Emeril's Essence Spice Mix, to taste

6 tablespoons olive oil

1 small onion, diced

6 garlic cloves, chopped

CREOLAISE SAUCE

2 egg yolks

1 teaspoon lemon juice

1/8 teaspoon cayenne pepper

2 teaspoons water

8 tablespoons butter, melted

1 tablespoon whole-grain mustard

2 teaspoons finely chopped fresh parsley

CORNY BREAD

1 box Jiffy corn bread mix

1 (7½-oz.) can whole kernel corn

1 (7½-oz.) can cream-style corn

1 cup sour cream

2 eggs, beaten

¼ cup sugar

8 tablespoons butter, melted

1 For Chicken: Generously sprinkle each breast with seasoning. Cover and refrigerate 30 minutes. Heat 4 tablespoons oil in large skillet over medium heat. Cook chicken until no longer pink in center, golden brown on both sides and juices run clear. Heat remaining oil in separate, small skillet and cook onion and garlic over medium-low heat until caramelized, being careful not to burn. Sprinkle mixture evenly over chicken.

2 For Sauce: In double boiler over simmering water, whisk egg yolks with the lemon juice, cayenne and water until pale yellow and slightly thick. Remove bowl from heat and whisking vigorously, add butter, 1 teaspoon at a time, until smooth. Stir in mustard and parsley; keep warm.

3 For Bread: Heat oven to 350°F. Lightly butter a deep 2- to 3-quart baking dish. Stir together corn bread mix, whole kernel corn, cream-style corn, sour cream, eggs, sugar and butter until moist. Pour into prepared baking dish. Bake 25 minutes or until toothpick inserted in center comes out clean. Cool slightly before removing from pan. Cut into 8 triangle-sized pieces.

4 To serve, place two pieces of bread on each serving plate with tips touching on one end and fanned apart leaving space in the middle for chicken breast. Drizzle Creolaise Sauce over chicken and Corny Bread.

4 servings.

Delightful Desserts

ALMOND CHERRY FLAVORED BISCOTTI

Stacia Chivilo, Indian Head Park, IL

5¼ cups all-purpose flour

5 teaspoons baking powder

2 cups sugar

1 cup butter, softened

6 eggs, beaten

1½ tablespoons almond extract

½ tablespoon vanilla extract

1½ cups dried tart cherries, slightly chopped

¾ cup almonds, coarsely chopped

1 Heat oven to 350°F.

2 Stir together flour and baking powder in large bowl. Stir together sugar and butter; add eggs and extracts and flour mixture and mix with a wooden spoon. Stir in cherries and nuts; dough will be soft. Divide dough into 3 equal parts. Shape into logs and place on 3 separate baking sheets (they will expand). Bake 20 minutes. Remove and let cool slightly. Cut into pieces and return to oven to toast. Drizzle top with a powdered sugar glaze, if desired.

24 to 36 servings.

SUPER EASY FUDGE

Michele Hayes, Nanaimo, BC, Canada

3 cups chocolate chips

1 (14-oz.) can sweetened condensed milk

¼ cup butter

Walnuts, if desired

1 Place chocolate chips, milk, butter and walnuts in medium microwavable dish. Cook on high 3 minutes, stirring every minute, until melted and smooth. Pour mixture into 8-inch-square baking dish. Cool and cut into squares.

16 servings.

LEMON PECAN BUTTER BALLS

Jill Wright, Dixon, IL

1 cup butter, softened

¼ cup sugar

1 teaspoon vanilla extract

1 tablespoon grated lemon peel

2 cups sifted all-purpose flour

1 cup chopped pecans

Sifted powdered sugar

1 Heat oven to 300°F. Line 2 baking sheets with parchment paper.

2 With spoon, cream together butter and sugar in large bowl until blended. Blend in vanilla and lemon peel. Stir in flour and pecans.

3 Shape into small balls, about 1 inch, and place 2 inches apart onto prepared baking sheets. Bake 20 minutes or until lightly browned. Cool on wire rack. When completely cool, roll in powdered sugar. Store in glass jar for at least one week before serving.

4 dozen.

FUDGEY COCOA NO-BAKES

Candace Brown, Vancouver, WA

2 cups sugar

½ cup butter, softened

½ cup milk

⅓ cup cocoa

3 cups quick-cooking oats

⅔ cup peanut butter

2 teaspoons vanilla extract

1 Stir together sugar, butter, milk and cocoa in large saucepan. Cook over medium heat, stirring constantly until boiling. Remove from heat; stir in oats, peanut butter and vanilla; stir until mix is combined. Drop by spoonfuls onto waxed paper and cool.

24 to 36 servings.

Lemon Pecan Butter Balls

BLACKBERRY COBBLER

Tamara Rossitto, Santa Rosa, CA

2 (16-oz.) bags frozen blackberries or marion berries

¼ cup sugar or to taste

1½ teaspoons ground cinnamon, divided

1 box pound cake mix

1 cup chopped pecans

½ cup butter, softened

1 Heat oven to 350°F. Butter 13x9-inch baking dish.

2 In large bowl, stir together blackberries, sugar and ½ teaspoon cinnamon. Spread evenly in baking dish.

3 In another large bowl, stir together cake mix, pecans and remaining cinnamon. With pastry blender, mix in butter until crumbly. Sprinkle evenly over blackberries. Bake 45 minutes to 1 hour or until bubbly and topping is golden brown. Serve warm with whipped cream or ice cream, if desired.

8 servings.

APPLE PECAN BUNDLES

Sandra Morgan, Summerville, SC

2 apples, peeled, quartered

1 (8-oz.) pkg. refrigerated crescent rolls, separated

1 cup packed brown sugar

Butter, to taste

2 tablespoons ground cinnamon

1 (5-oz.) bag pecans

1 (12-oz.) can Mountain Dew

1 Heat oven to 350°F. Place one apple piece in each crescent and roll up. Repeat and place in 13x9-inch baking dish. Melt brown sugar, butter and cinnamon in medium saucepan. Stir in pecans. Pour over crescent rolls. Pour Mountain Dew over top. Bake 30 to 35 minutes.

6 to 8 servings.

LIES' FRIENDSHIP COOKIES

Lies Vanbergen, Woodstock, ON, Canada

1 lb. butter, softened

2 cups packed brown sugar

2 cups sugar

5 eggs

2 teaspoons vanilla extract

4 cups all-purpose flour

1 teaspoon salt

2 teaspoons baking soda

2 teaspoons baking powder

5 cups oatmeal, finely chopped in a food processor

3½ oz. white chocolate, grated

3½ oz. milk chocolate, grated

3½ oz. bittersweet chocolate, grated

3 cups semisweet chocolate chips

1 cup chopped walnuts

1 cup chopped pecans

1 cup chopped almonds

1 Heat oven to 375°F.

2 Stir together butter and sugar until combined in large bowl. Stir in eggs and extract until combined. Slowly stir in flour.

3 In separate medium bowl, stir together the salt, baking soda, baking powder and oatmeal and slowly add to flour mixture. Stir together all grated chocolate, chocolate chips and nuts and add to flour mixture, mixing until well combined.

4 Form tablespoon-sized balls and place 2 inches apart on baking sheets. Bake 12 minutes. (Cookies do not look done but do not overbake them.) Leave cookies on baking sheets 5 minutes before transferring to a wire cooling rack.

7 to 8 dozen.

MONSTER COOKIES

Angie Liddiard, Tooele, UT

    3 eggs

    1¼ cups packed light brown sugar

    1 cup sugar

    ½ teaspoon salt

    ½ teaspoon vanilla extract

    2 teaspoons baking soda

    1½ cups creamy peanut butter

    1 stick butter, melted

    1 cup chocolate chips

    4½ cups quick-cooking oatmeal

1 Heat oven to 350°F. Line baking sheets with parchment paper.

2 In very large mixing bowl, stir together eggs and sugars. Stir in salt, vanilla, baking soda, peanut butter and butter until thoroughly combined. Stir in chocolate chips and oatmeal.

3 Drop by tablespoonfuls, 2 inches apart onto prepared baking sheets. Bake 6 to 7 minutes. Do not overbake. Remove parchment sheet with cookies onto counter or cooling racks to cool. Store in airtight container.

4 to 6 servings.

TASTY ICE CREAM SANDWICHES

Teresa Williams, DeRidder, LA

    1 (15-oz.) box chocolate graham crackers, halved

    1 (8-oz.) container frozen fat-free whipped topping, thawed

1 Spread half the crackers with 2 tablespoons whipped topping. Gently press remaining crackers on top, forming a sandwich. Place on baking sheets in single layer and freeze 2 hours. Wrap each sandwich in waxed paper to store frozen.

12 to 16 servings.

EASY NO-BAKE COOKIES

Clare Morgan-Heupel, Duluth, MN

    ¼ cup butter

    2 cups sugar

    6 tablespoons high quality cocoa

    ½ cup milk

    ½ cup creamy or chunky peanut butter

    ½ teaspoon vanilla extract

    3 cups old-fashioned oatmeal

    1 cup coconut

    Dash salt

1 Over medium heat, stir together butter, sugar, cocoa and milk in medium saucepan. Bring to full hard boil and continue to stir while boiling for 2 minutes. (This step is very important. Do not stop when it comes to a boil.) Remove from heat and stir in peanut butter, vanilla, oatmeal, coconut and salt. Drop by spoonfuls onto parchment paper and let set.

Servings vary.

POACHED APPLES OR PEARS

Angelana Cristan, Marquette, MI

    4 cups water

    4 cups white wine

    3 cups sugar

    4 tablespoons vanilla extract

    Juice and peel of 4 lemons

    6 to 8 apples, peeled, cored or unpeeled, cored pears

1 In large saucepan, stir together water, white wine, sugar, vanilla, juice and peel; bring to a boil then reduce heat so liquid is barely simmering. Add apples to simmering liquid; cook 12 to 15 minutes or until apples are crisp-tender. Refrigerate, covered, overnight. Reheat in cooking liquid.

6 to 8 servings.

Fat Tuesday Bars

FAT TUESDAY BARS

DJ Laake, Estherville, IA

1 (18¼-oz.) German chocolate cake mix

1 (18¼-oz.) sour cream white cake mix

4 eggs

1 cup vegetable oil

⅓ cup chopped pecans

¼ cup dark chocolate chips

¼ cup semisweet chocolate chips

¾ cup shredded coconut

1 (7-oz.) jar marshmallow cream

1 Heat oven to 350°F.

2 Stir together cake mixes, eggs and oil in large bowl until combined. Pour half of the batter into 13x9-inch ungreased pan. Bake 12 to 15 minutes. Top with pecans, chocolate chips, coconut and marshmallow cream. Drop remaining batter over the top and bake an additional 15 to 20 minutes. Allow to cool before cutting.

24 servings.

CANDY "SUSHI"

Brian Redman, Louisville, KY

1 tablespoon butter

12 large marshmallows

2 cups crispy rice cereal

1 box cherry or strawberry flavored fruit roll-ups

1 bag red licorice whips

1 bag black licorice whips

1 In large saucepan, melt butter over low heat. Stir in marshmallows until melted. Stir in cereal until well coated; remove from heat. Unroll fruit roll-ups. Place 2 to 3 tablespoons cereal mixture on one side. Lay licorice whips on top and roll up tightly. Slice with a serrated knife; repeat if desired. Roll fruit roll-ups with cereal, slice and tie with black licorice to create "seaweed."

24 to 36 servings.

PERSIMMON COOKIES

Dorothy Anderson, Sacramento, CA

1 cup persimmon pulp, beaten

1 teaspoon baking soda

1 cup sugar

½ cup shortening

1 egg, beaten

2 cups all-purpose flour

1 teaspoon ground cinnamon

½ teaspoon ground cloves

½ teaspoon ground nutmeg

½ teaspoon salt

1 cup chopped walnuts

1 cup raisins

1 Heat oven to 375°F. Spray baking sheet with cooking spray.

2 Sprinkle permission pulp with baking soda in large bowl. Beat together sugar and shortening until creamy; add egg and persimmon pulp and beat until combined. Sift together flour and spices and add to sugar mixture until combined. Stir in nuts and raisins. Drop by tablespoons onto prepared baking sheet. Bake 12 to 15 minutes.

3 dozen.

RAISIN-NUT-OATMEAL COOKIES

Kathy Allred, Tucson, AZ

$3/4$ cup butter

1 cup Splenda sugar substitute or sugar

$1/2$ cup packed brown sugar

$1/4$ cup milk or $1/3$ cup soy milk

1 egg

1 teaspoon vanilla extract

1 cup all-purpose flour

1 teaspoon ground cinnamon

$1/4$ teaspoon ground nutmeg

$1/2$ teaspoon baking soda

$1/4$ teaspoon salt

3 cups old-fashioned rolled oats

$1/2$ cup raisins

$1/2$ cup chopped walnuts

1 Heat oven to 350°F. Spray baking sheet with cooking spray.

2 Beat butter and Splenda in large bowl on medium speed until fluffy. Add brown sugar, milk, egg and vanilla; mix until combined.

3 Stir together flour, cinnamon, nutmeg, baking soda and salt in medium bowl; add to sugar mixture to combine. Stir in rolled oats, raisins and walnuts. Drop by tablespoonfuls onto prepared baking sheet and flatten, if necessary. Bake 12 to 15 minutes; cool on wire rack.

3 dozen.

FROSTED BANANA BARS

Candace Brown, Vancouver, WA

BARS

$1/2$ cup butter, softened

2 cups sugar

3 eggs

$1 1/2$ cups mashed bananas (about 3 medium)

1 teaspoon vanilla or almond extract

2 cups all-purpose flour

1 teaspoon baking soda

Dash salt

FROSTING

$1/2$ cup butter, softened

1 (8-oz.) pkg. cream cheese, softened

4 cups powdered sugar

2 teaspoons vanilla or almond extract

1 For Bars: Heat oven to 375°F. Spray 15x10x1-inch baking pan with cooking spray. In large mixing bowl, cream butter and sugar. Beat in eggs, bananas and vanilla. In medium bowl, combine flour, baking soda and salt; add to creamed mixture and mix well. Pour into prepared baking pan and bake 25 minutes or until toothpick inserted in center comes out clean; cool.

2 For Frosting: Cream butter and cream cheese together in large bowl. Gradually add powdered sugar and vanilla; beat well. Spread over cooled bars and cut.

24 servings.

MY OWN VANILLA COOKIES

Susan Pacenza, Nineveh, NY

> 1 cup butter
>
> 1 cup sugar
>
> 2 eggs
>
> 1 teaspoon baking powder
>
> 1 teaspoon vanilla extract
>
> Dash salt
>
> 2½ cups all-purpose flour

1 Heat oven to 350°F. Spray baking sheet with cooking spray.

2 Stir together butter, sugar, eggs, baking powder, vanilla, salt and flour in large bowl with wooden spoon until combined. Bake on greased baking sheet for 10 minutes.

3 to 4 dozen.

CALVARY DESSERT

Pat Clevenger, Parma Heights, OH

> 1 (3-oz.) pkg. orange gelatin Jello
>
> 1 (20-oz.) can crushed pineapple in juice, drained, juice reserved
>
> 1 (4-serving size) pkg. vanilla pudding
>
> 2 cups milk
>
> 1 cup heavy whipping cream, whipped

1 Make Jello according to package directions using reserved pineapple juice as part of the cold water; let set in refrigerator.

2 In medium bowl, prepare pudding according to package directions.

3 When Jello is set, whip with wire whisk. Fold in crushed pineapple and pudding to whipped Jello. Fold in whipped cream.

10 to 12 servings.

PUMPKIN BARS

Asia Vanatta, West Linn, OR

BARS

> ¾ cup butter
>
> 2 cups sugar
>
> 4 eggs, beaten
>
> 1 (15-oz.) can pumpkin puree
>
> 2 cups all-purpose flour
>
> 2 teaspoons baking powder
>
> ½ teaspoon baking soda
>
> ½ teaspoon salt
>
> 1 teaspoon ground cinnamon
>
> 1 teaspoon pumpkin pie spice
>
> 1 cup chopped walnuts, if desired

FROSTING

> 1 (3-oz.) pkg. cream cheese, softened
>
> ⅓ cup butter, softened
>
> 1 teaspoon vanilla extract
>
> 3 cups sifted powdered sugar

1 For Bars: Heat oven to 350°F. Butter and flour 10x15-inch jelly-roll pan. In large bowl, cream together ¾ cup butter and sugar until light and fluffy. Beat in eggs one at a time and stir in pumpkin puree. In another large bowl, combine flour, baking powder, baking soda, salt, cinnamon and pumpkin pie spice; stir into pumpkin mixture. Stir in walnuts. Spread evenly in prepared pan. Bake 30 to 35 minutes or until toothpick inserted near the center comes out clean. Cool completely before frosting.

2 For Frosting: In medium bowl mix together cream cheese, ⅓ cup butter and vanilla until smooth. Gradually blend in powdered sugar and beat until smooth. Spread over cooled pumpkin bars. Cut into squares.

24 servings.

S'MORE BARS

Candace Brown, Vancouver, WA

½ cup butter

¼ cup packed brown sugar

1 teaspoon vanilla extract

2 cups graham cracker crumbs

2 cups miniature marshmallows

4 (1.55-oz.) milk chocolate candy bars

1 Heat oven to 250°F. Line 8x8-inch square pan with buttered aluminum foil.

2 In medium saucepan, combine butter and brown sugar. Cook over medium heat until sugar dissolves and mixture is bubbly. Stir in vanilla, cracker crumbs and marshmallows. Cook and stir just until marshmallows begin to melt. Spread evenly into prepared pan. With back of a large buttered spoon, press mixture into pan to make an even layer. Set candy bars, side by side, in a single layer to cover top. Place in oven 5 minutes until chocolate is shiny all over. With spatula, spread chocolate evenly over top. Refrigerate. Cut into bars.

16 bars.

BROWN BEAR MILKSHAKE

Tommy Roman, Aberdeen, WA

1½ fresh vanilla beans, halved

2 cups half-and-half

1½ tablespoons shredded coconut

1 tablespoon ground cinnamon

½ teaspoon ground nutmeg

2 to 2½ scoops dark chocolate ice cream

1 In medium bowl, scrape vanilla beans into half-and-half; stir and let steep in refrigerator overnight. Add shredded coconut, cinnamon and nutmeg to half-and-half mixture; let stand 15 minutes to blend flavors. Place in blender with ice cream and pulse to desired thickness.

2 servings.

APPLE CRISP

Alice Grove, Bethel, OH

6 cups Granny Smith apples, peeled, sliced

1 cup packed dark brown sugar

¾ cup oats

1 teaspoon ground cinnamon

½ teaspoon ground nutmeg

½ cup butter, softened

1 Heat oven to 375°F. Spray 8- or 9-inch square baking dish with cooking spray.

2 In large bowl, stir together apples, brown sugar, oats, cinnamon, nutmeg and butter until mixture is crumbly. Sprinkle over apples. Bake 35 to 40 minutes or until topping is golden brown and bubbling. Serve warm with vanilla ice cream, if desired.

8 to 10 servings.

MANGO ICE CREAM

Pallavi Belamkar, Carmel, IN

2½ cups milk

1½ cups half-and-half

½ cup sugar

2 large mangoes, peeled, chopped

2 tablespoons sugar

1 In large saucepan, cook milk, half-and-half and ½ cup sugar over medium heat, stirring occasionally until reduced by one third; cool completely.

2 Puree mango chunks in blender; strain.

3 Place mangoes and 2 tablespoons sugar in large, nonstick skillet. Cook, stirring constantly, until thickened; cool completely. Combine both and process in an ice cream machine 25 to 30 minutes. Pour into large, freezer-safe bowl; cover and let set. Serve with strawberry halves as garnish, if desired.

8 to 10 servings.

Apple Crisp

TURTLE BARS

Ann Stock, St. Charles, MO

1 (18¼-oz.) German chocolate cake mix

¾ cup butter, melted

⅓ cup evaporated milk

1 (12-oz.) bag semisweet chocolate chips

1 (12-oz.) jar caramel topping

1 Heat oven to 350°F. Spray 13x9-inch baking dish with cooking spray.

2 Mix together cake mix, butter and evaporated milk in large bowl. Spread half of brownie mixture into prepared pan; pat until flat. Bake 15 minutes. Pour chocolate chips and caramel over brownie mixture. Top with remaining brownie mix and pat until flat. Bake an additional 25 to 30 minutes. Cool in refrigerator before cutting.

24 servings.

PEACH ENCHILADAS

Lisa Haycraft, Stuart, VA

2 (8-oz.) pkgs. refrigerated crescent rolls, separated

4 peaches, peeled, quartered (or very well drained canned peaches)

1 cup better, melted

1½ cups sugar

1 tablespoon ground cinnamon

1 (12-oz.) can Mountain Dew

1 Heat oven to 350°F.

2 Place peach quarter on each roll; roll up. Place crescent rolls in 13x9-inch baking dish.

3 In medium bowl, stir together butter, sugar and cinnamon; pour over crescent rolls. Pour Mountain Dew over all. Bake 25 minutes or until golden brown.

6 to 8 servings.

ANISETTE FLAVORED BISCOTTI

Stacia Chivilo, Indian Head Park, IL

5 cups all-purpose flour

5 teaspoons baking powder

2 cups sugar

1 cup butter, softened

6 eggs, beaten

2 teaspoons anise oil

1 Heat oven to 350°F.

2 Combine flour and baking power in medium bowl; set aside. By hand, combine sugar, butter, eggs and anise oil in large bowl. Stir in the flour mixture with a wooden spoon; dough will be soft. Divide dough into 3 equal parts and shape into logs. Place on 3 separate baking sheets (they will expand). Bake 20 minutes. Remove and, while still warm, cut into pieces and return to oven to toast.

24 to 36 servings.

APRICOT PEARS

Dorothy Miller, Madison, WI

6 Bosc pears, peeled, cored

12 dried Turkish apricots

¾ cup apricot jam

3 tablespoons fresh lemon juice

Sweetened whipped cream, if desired

1 Cut off bottom of pears to provide level base. Insert 2 apricots into each pear.

2 In small microwavable bowl, melt jam in microwave about 1½ minutes. Stir in lemon juice. Spoon mixture over pears. Place upright in a shallow bowl; cover tightly with microwave-safe plastic wrap. Microwave 12 minutes on high or until pears are soft. Serve with a dollop of unsweetened whipped cream, if desired.

6 servings.

POACHED PEARS IN CHOCOLATE AMARETTO SAUCE

Brenda Haley, Thorsby, AB, Canada

2 cups red wine

2 cups grape juice

1 cinnamon stick

4 pears, peeled, cored

200 grams (7 oz.) semisweet or bittersweet chocolate, or burnt chocolate almond bars

2 tablespoons butter

2 to 4 tablespoons Amaretto liqueur

1 In medium saucepan, bring wine, grape juice and cinnamon stick to a boil. Reduce heat to simmer.

2 Meanwhile trim bottoms of pears to stand up in serving dish. Add pears to simmering pan; cover and cook until just tender, about 10 minutes. Remove, and chill.

3 Melt chocolate and butter in microwavable-safe dish on low setting. Stir in Amaretto. Pour chocolate over top of pears.

4 servings.

THE NO NAME TREAT

Juliet Murray, Houston, TX

1 (11.5- to 12-oz.) bag chocolate chips

1 (11.5- to 12-oz.) bag peanut butter chips

1 (11.5- to 12-oz.) bag butterscotch chips

1 (11.5-oz.) bag potato chips, crushed

Nuts, if desired

1 In large microwavable bowl, melt all three chips on high heat. Stir potato chips and nuts into chocolate mixture until well coated. Form mixture into balls; refrigerate until hardened.

16 to 24 servings.

PEACH SURPRISE

Peggy M. Yamaguchi-Lazar, Eugene, OR

1½ cups small pretzels, crushed

½ cup butter, melted

1 cup sugar, divided

1 (8-oz.) pkg. cream cheese, softened

1 (8-oz.) container frozen whipped topping, thawed

1 (6-oz.) pkg. peach flavored gelatin

2 (10-oz.) cans peaches, drained, juice reserved or 1½ quarts fresh peaches

1 Heat oven to 325°F.

2 In medium bowl, mix crushed pretzels, melted butter and ½ cup sugar. Press mixture into 13x9-inch baking dish. Bake 6 minutes; cool.

3 In another medium bowl, stir together cream cheese, whipped topping and remaining sugar. Spread on top of pretzels layer.

4 In large bowl, mix gelatin with reserved juice and enough boiling water to make 2 cups; stir until thickened. Stir in fruit. Pour gelatin mixture over top of cream cheese layer; chill. Store in refrigerator.

16 servings.

PEANUT BUTTER COOKIES

Misty Lianos, Eagleville, TN

1 cup peanut butter

1 cup sugar

1 egg

1 Heat oven to 350°F.

2 Stir together peanut butter, sugar and egg in large bowl until combined. Shape into round balls and place on parchment-lined baking sheet; press with floured fork and bake 9 minutes. Let cool on baking sheet for 10 minutes; Remove to wire rack.

2 dozen.

WHITE CHOCOLATE ALMOND BARS

Roselyn Shiver, Knoxville, TN

1 (18½-oz.) box white cake mix

½ cup butter, softened

1 egg

½ cup toasted sliced almonds, finely chopped

1 (12-oz.) container vanilla frosting

1½ cups white chocolate chips

1 cup toasted sliced almonds

1 cup coconut flakes

1 Heat oven to 400°F. Line 13x9-inch pan with aluminum foil, leaving 1 inch extra on each end. Lightly spray foil with cooking spray.

2 Beat cake mix, butter, egg and almonds in large bowl until soft dough forms; pat evenly into prepared pan. Bake until light golden brown, about 15 to 20 minutes. Cool on rack 5 to 10 minutes. Turn oven to broil. Spread frosting onto cake. Sprinkle with white chocolate chips, almonds and coconut. Broil until coconut is golden brown. Remove; cool completely. Cut into 1½ x 2-inch bars.

2 dozen.

PEANUT BUTTER CUPS

Ann Stock, St. Charles, MO

1 lb. powdered sugar

1 cup butter, melted

1½ cups peanut butter

1¼ cups graham cracker crumbs

1 (12-oz.) pkg. semisweet chocolate chips

1 Stir together powdered sugar, butter, peanut butter and cracker crumbs in large bowl. Press into 13x9-inch baking dish. Melt chocolate chips and spread over peanut butter mixture. Refrigerate and cut into squares to serve.

24 servings.

STRAWBERRY SHORTCAKE ICE CREAM

Elaine Sweet, Dallas, TX

2½ cups half-and-half

4 eggs, beaten

1 cup sugar

1 (8-oz.) pkg. cream cheese, cubed and softened

3 cups strawberries, finely chopped

2 tablespoons fresh lemon juice

2 tablespoons vanilla extract

3 cups whipping cream

1 (14-oz.) can condensed milk

1 cup granola cereal, finely ground

½ cup chopped almonds

½ cup melted butter

1 In small saucepan, combine half-and-half, eggs and sugar with a wire whisk. Cook and stir over medium heat until thick and bubbly, about 12 minutes. Remove from heat and refrigerate 1 hour.

2 In large bowl, beat cream cheese until smooth; gradually beat into chilled egg mixture. Fold in strawberries, lemon juice, vanilla, whipping cream and condensed milk; stir well until combined. Cover and refrigerate. Pour mixture into ice cream freezer and freeze according to directions.

3 Place granola and almonds on baking sheet; drizzle with butter and place in 350°F oven to toast and lightly brown, about 10 minutes. Scoop ice cream into serving bowls and top with crunch topping.

6 to 8 servings.

Dessert Traditions

APPLE PIE

Beth Bangert, Delano, MN

10 to 12 cups sliced apples

1½ cups sugar

¼ teaspoon salt

2½ teaspoons baking spice

½ teaspoon orange peel or ¼ teaspoon powdered orange peel

¼ teaspoon orange extract

2 tablespoons clear gel

½ cup water, orange juice or apple juice

1 tablespoon milk

1 tablespoon cream

2 tablespoons butter

2 (9-inch) prepared pie crusts

Coarse sugar

1 Place apples in large bowl of salted water to prevent browning; drain. Stir together sugar, salt, baking spice, orange peel, orange extract and clear gel in large bowl. Stir in water, milk and cream; pour over apples and stir until apples are well coated.

2 Heat oven to 400°F.

3 Fill pie shell with apple mixture, heaping apples in the center. Wet rim of bottom crust and dot apples with butter. Drape top crust over filling and press onto bottom rim. Trim within ½ inch and fold under bottom crust; pinch and flute edges. Cut steam vent. Use extra dough to make cutouts for decoration on top crust such as folk heart small cookie cutter marking each slice. Bake 40 minutes. Remove and baste crust with milk and sprinkle with coarse sugar. Return to oven and continue baking until golden brown and bubbling in the center. Cover rim of crust with foil if pie begins to brown too much. Let cool to room temperature before cutting.

8 to 12 servings.

DOUBLE LAYER PUMPKIN PIE

Ann Kerttula, Norwich, CT

4 oz. cream cheese, softened

1 tablespoon sugar

1 cup plus 1 tablespoon milk, divided

1 (8-oz.) container whipped topping, thawed, divided

1 (9-inch) graham-cracker pie crust

1 (15-oz.) can pumpkin

2 (4-serving size each) pkgs. vanilla pudding mix

1 teaspoon ground cinnamon

½ teaspoon ground ginger

¼ teaspoon ground cloves

1 Whisk together cream cheese, sugar and 1 tablespoon milk in large bowl with wire whisk until well blended. Fold in half of the whipped topping. Spread into prepared pie crust. Pour 1 cup milk into large bowl; whisk in pumpkin, pudding mixes and spices. Beat with wire whisk 2 minutes or until well blended and thickened. Spread over cream cheese layer. Refrigerate 4 hours or until set. Store in refrigerator.

1 pie.

SCRUMPTIOUS CHOCOLATE CAKE

Sandra Kupchin, Brooklyn, NY

2 cups all-purpose flour

1 cup sugar

½ cup cocoa

1 cup shortening

Dash salt

1¼ cups orange juice

½ teaspoon baking powder

1½ teaspoons baking soda

3 eggs

½ cup shortening

1 teaspoon vanilla extract

1 Heat oven to 350°F.

2 In large bowl, mix together flour, sugar, cocoa, shortening and salt on medium speed until combined. Add orange juice, baking powder, baking soda, eggs, shortening and vanilla and mix on medium speed 2 minutes. Pour into 13x9-inch pan and bake 45 minutes.

10 to 12 servings.

QUICK CITRUS PIE

Sylvia Stevenson, Black River, MI

1 (8-oz.) pkg. cream cheese, softened

1 (14-oz.) can sweetened condensed milk

4 oz. key lime puree

8 oz. heavy whipping cream, whipped

1 (9-inch) prepared graham-cracker crust

1 Whip cream cheese in large bowl on medium speed until creamy. Slowly add condensed milk. Add lime puree. Fold in whipped cream; pour into crust. Chill at least 2 hours or overnight.

1 pie.

CARROT CAKE WITH CREAM FROSTING

Anna J. Ibeling, Sherburn, MN

CAKE

¼ cup apple butter with cinnamon

¼ cup vegetable oil

7 eggs

2 teaspoons vanilla extract

1¼ cups self-rising flour

¾ cup sugar substitute

3 tablespoons pumpkin pie spice

1 cup shredded carrots

¼ cup seedless raisins

¼ cup crushed pineapple, well drained

FROSTING

2 oz. reduced-fat cream cheese, softened

2 tablespoons butter, softened

½ teaspoon vanilla extract

1 cup powdered sugar

1 For Cake: Heat oven to 350°F. Spray 8-inch square pan with cooking spray. Beat apple butter, oil, eggs and vanilla with electric mixer on medium speed until well blended. Stir in flour, sugar substitute and pumpkin pie spice. Fold in carrots, raisins and pineapple until blended. Spread batter into prepared pan. Bake 30 to 35 minutes or until toothpick inserted in center comes out clean. Cool on wire rack.

2 For Frosting: Beat cream cheese and butter with electric mixer on medium speed until well blended; stir in vanilla. Gradually beat in powdered sugar until light and fluffy.

12 servings.

APPLESAUCE CHOCOLATE CHIP CAKE

Cathy Miller, Hanover, PA

1 cup vegetable oil

2 cups sugar

2 eggs

2 cups applesauce

3½ cups all-purpose flour

3 teaspoons baking powder

2 teaspoons vanilla extract

2 teaspoons cinnamon

1 teaspoon ground cloves

1 teaspoon baking soda

½ teaspoon salt

2 cups mini chocolate chips

❶ Heat oven to 350°F.

❷ Stir together oil, sugar, eggs, applesauce, flour, baking powder, vanilla, cinnamon, cloves, baking soda and salt in large bowl with wooden spoon. Stir in chocolate chips and spoon into 13x9-inch pan. Bake 1 hour or until toothpick inserted in center comes out clean.

10 to 12 servings.

GRANNY'S FANCY TARTS

Hope Wasylenki, Gahanna, OH

4 cups all-purpose flour

1 tablespoon sugar

1 teaspoon salt

1 teaspoon baking powder

1½ cups lard or 1½ cups plus 1 tablespoon vegetable shortening

1 egg, beaten

1 tablespoon lemon juice

½ cup ice water

1 egg

1 cup packed brown sugar

1 teaspoon vanilla extract

1 tablespoon butter, softened

1 cup golden raisins

1 cup coconut

1 cup chopped walnuts

❶ Sift together flour, sugar, salt and baking powder in large bowl; cut in vegetable shortening with pastry blender until mixture resembles coarse crumbs. Stir in egg, lemon juice and water. Pat into circle; let rest 15 minutes. Cut dough into 4 pieces, patting each into a circle.

❷ Heat oven to 375°F.

❸ Cut circles from pie dough with a biscuit cutter or small round cookie cutter. Depending on the size of the circles, fit into either a mini-muffin pan or a regular-sized muffin pan.

❹ Using hand mixer or wooden spoon, blend egg, sugar, vanilla and butter in large bowl. Fold in raisins, coconut and walnuts. For mini tarts, use a teaspoon to drop filling into dough. For larger tarts, use 2 teaspoonfuls. Bake 15 minutes or until browned.

Servings vary.

Granny's Fancy Tarts

BANANA NUT CAKE

Dorothy Anderson, Sacramento, CA

CAKE

½ lb. butter, softened

1 cup sugar

2 eggs

2 cups cake flour

2 teaspoons baking powder

½ teaspoon baking soda

¼ cup milk or ⅓ cup buttermilk or soured cream

⅔ cup mashed ripe bananas

¼ cup chopped pecans or walnuts

ICING

¼ cup mashed ripe bananas

2 teaspoons lemon juice

¼ teaspoon vanilla extract

2 cups sifted powdered sugar

1 For Cake: Heat oven to 325°F. Grease and flour 9-inch pan. In large bowl, cream butter until creamy. Add sugar, a small amount at a time. When well blended, add eggs, one at a time, and beat 3 to 4 minutes on high speed. Sift together flour, baking powder and baking soda in medium bowl. With wooden spoon, stir in milk, bananas and nuts. Pour into prepared pan. Bake 45 minutes. Increase temperature to 375°F and bake an additional 7 to 8 minutes or until golden brown. Cool.

2 For Icing: Place bananas, lemon juice and vanilla in large bowl and beat with electric mixer on medium speed until smooth. Add sugar to desired consistency. Spread mixture over cake. Let set 15 minutes; cut into squares.

Servings vary.

CARAMEL NUT CAKE

Brenda Melancon, Sorrento, LA

1 (18.25-oz.) box yellow cake mix

⅓ cup butter, softened

⅓ cup water

⅓ cup caramel-flavored ice cream topping

4 eggs

1 cup finely chopped pecans

1 cup milk chocolate and caramel swirled morsels

1 cup shredded coconut

Caramel topping

1 Heat oven to 350°F. Lightly grease and flour 10-inch Bundt pan.

2 In large bowl, combine cake mix, butter, water and topping. Beat with an electric mixer on low speed until blended. Add eggs; increase mixer speed to medium and beat 2 minutes. Stir in pecans, chocolate morsels and coconut. Spoon mixture evenly into prepared pan. Bake 40 to 50 minutes or until toothpick inserted near center comes out clean. Cool in pan 15 minutes. Invert cake onto a serving platter. While warm, drizzle with caramel topping.

10 servings.

CARROT CAKE WITH CREAM CHEESE FROSTING

Donna Gray, Blue Hill, ME

CAKE

2 cups all-purpose flour

2 teaspoons baking powder

1½ teaspoons baking soda

1½ teaspoons salt

2 teaspoons ground cinnamon

2 cups sugar

1½ cups vegetable oil

4 eggs

½ cup chopped walnuts

2 cups grated carrots

3 oz. flaked coconut

1 (8½-oz.) can crushed pineapple

FROSTING

½ cup butter, softened

1 (8-oz.) pkg. cream cheese, softened

1 teaspoon vanilla extract

16 oz. powdered sugar

Milk, if desired

1 For Cake: Heat oven to 350°F. Grease and flour 3 (9-inch) round cake pans. Sift together flour, baking powder, baking soda, salt and cinnamon in large bowl; add sugar and mix well. Stir in oil and eggs and mix well. Add nuts, grated carrots, coconut and pineapple; mix well. Pour into prepared pans. Bake 35 to 40 minutes or until toothpick inserted in center comes out clean; cool on wire rack.

2 For Frosting: Beat butter, cream cheese, vanilla extract and powdered sugar together in medium bowl until smooth. Add a small amount of milk to desired consistency.

10 to 12 servings.

APPLE CAKE

Randee Eckstein, Commack, NY

4 tablespoons butter or margarine, softened

1 cup plus 2 tablespoons sugar, divided

3 eggs

2 cups self-rising flour

1 cup sour cream or plain yogurt

1 teaspoon vanilla extract

1 teaspoon cinnamon

¼ teaspoon ground nutmeg

⅛ teaspoon ground cloves

2 Granny Smith apples, peeled, chopped

1 cup chopped walnuts

1 Heat oven to 350°F. Grease and flour 8x10-inch loaf pan or 9-inch square pan.

2 In large bowl, cream butter and 1 cup sugar. Add eggs one at a time, mixing well after each addition. Mix in flour alternating with sour cream. Stir in vanilla.

3 Mix 2 tablespoons sugar and spices in small bowl. Pour half the batter into prepared pan. Spread apples over batter. Sprinkle with half of sugar, spice mixture. Spoon on remaining batter, covering apples. Sprinkle with walnuts and remaining sugar, spice mixture.

4 If using a loaf pan, bake 1 hour or until toothpick inserted in center comes out clean. If using square pan, bake 30 to 40 minutes or until toothpick inserted in center comes out clean.

10 to 12 servings.

Sky-High Strawberry Pie

SKY–HIGH STRAWBERRY PIE

Linda Murray, Allenstown, NH

3 quarts strawberries, divided

1½ cups sugar

6 tablespoons cornstarch

⅔ cup water

Red food coloring, if desired

1 (10-inch) deep-dish pastry shell, baked

1 cup whipping cream

1½ tablespoons instant vanilla pudding mix

1 In large bowl, mash enough strawberries to equal 3 cups.

2 In large saucepan, combine sugar and cornstarch over medium heat. Stir in mashed berries and water; mix well. Bring to a boil, stirring constantly. Cook and stir 2 minutes. Remove from heat; add food coloring, if desired. Pour into large bowl; refrigerate 20 minutes, stirring occasionally, until mixture is lukewarm. Fold in remaining berries. Pour into prepared pie shell. Refrigerate 2 to 3 hours until set.

3 In small bowl, whip cream until soft peaks form. Sprinkle pudding mix over cream and whip until stiff; serve with the pie. Refrigerate leftovers.

8 to 10 servings.

HO HO CAKE

Ann Stock, St. Charles, MO

CAKE

1 box chocolate cake mix

1¼ cups milk

5 tablespoons all-purpose flour

8 tablespoons butter, softened

1 cup shortening

1 cup sugar

FROSTING

8 tablespoons butter

4 oz. German semisweet chocolate

1 pasteurized egg

1 teaspoon vanilla extract

3 cups powdered sugar

2½ tablespoons water

1 For Cake: Bake cake mix according to directions in 11x15-inch jelly-roll pan; cool. Stir together milk and flour in medium saucepan over medium heat until thickened. Chill. Beat butter, shortening and sugar in large bowl until creamy; stir into chilled mixture. Spread over cooled cake.

2 For Topping: Melt butter and chocolate in medium saucepan over low heat. Remove from heat and stir in egg, vanilla, sugar and water until creamy. Spread over top of cream filling. Refrigerate until set.

16 to 24 servings.

MOM WILL'S WALNUT CAKE

Barbara Hamilton, Pompton Lakes, NJ

1 cup shortening

2 cups sugar

4 eggs

2 teaspoons vanilla extract

1 teaspoon baking soda

1 teaspoon baking powder

½ teaspoon salt

3 cups all-purpose flour

1 cup milk

1 cup ground walnuts

Powdered sugar, if desired

1 Heat oven to 350°F. Grease and flour 10-inch Bundt pan.

2 In large bowl, cream shortening and sugar. Add eggs and beat well. Blend in vanilla.

3 In separate medium bowl, mix baking soda, baking powder, salt and flour. Add to shortening mixture and blend. Gradually stir in milk and ground walnuts; blend thoroughly. Bake 1 hour. Cool on wire rack until sides of cake loosen from pan; remove and cool completely. Sprinkle with powdered sugar before serving.

16 servings.

STRAWBERRY TUNNEL CREAM CAKE

Amber Evans, Minneapolis, MN

1 (10-inch) prepared angel food cake

2 (3-oz.) pkgs. cream cheese, softened

1 (14-oz.) can sweetened condensed milk

⅓ cup lemon juice concentrate

1 teaspoon almond extract

2 to 4 drops red food coloring, if desired

1 cup chopped fresh strawberries

1 (12-oz.) container frozen whipped topping, thawed

1 Invert cake onto serving plate. Cut 1-inch slice crosswise from the top of the cake; set aside.

2 With sharp knife, cut around the cake about ½ inch from the center hole and about ½ inch from the outer edge. Remove the cake from the center of cuts leaving enough cake on the bottom to form a base. Reserve cake pieces.

3 In large bowl, beat cream cheese with electric mixer until fluffy. Gradually beat in sweetened condensed milk until smooth. Stir in lemon juice, almond extract and food coloring. Stir in reserved torn cake pieces and chopped strawberries. Fold in 1 cup whipped topping. Fill cavity of cake with the mixture; replace top cake slice. Chill 3 hours or until set. Frost cake with remaining whipped topping. Store in refrigerator.

10 to 12 servings.

SUGARLESS CAKE

Mable Watson, Lenoir, NC

1 cup hot water

½ cup shortening

1 cup molasses

2 eggs

1 teaspoon vanilla extract

2¼ cups all-purpose flour

¾ cup cocoa

2 teaspoons baking soda

½ teaspoon salt

1 Heat oven to 350°F. Grease 13x9-inch pan.

2 Stir together hot water, shortening, and molasses in large bowl. Add eggs and mix. Stir in vanilla.

3 In medium bowl, mix flour, cocoa, baking soda and salt. Add shortening mixture, stirring until blended. Pour into prepared pan. Bake until golden brown.

10 to 12 servings.

CHESS PIE

Michelle Walker, Brandon, FL

1 (9-inch) prepared pie crust

3 eggs

1 cup sugar

1 cup packed brown sugar

½ cup butter, melted

1 teaspoon vanilla extract

2 tablespoons all-purpose flour

1 cup whipping cream

1 teaspoon grated orange or lemon peel

1 Heat oven to 400°F. Prepare crust in 9-inch pie pan. In large bowl beat eggs until fluffy; beat in sugars gradually and add butter. Beat in vanilla, flour and cream. Mix well. Spoon into prepared crust. Sprinkle with grated peel. Bake 10 minutes; reduce oven temperature to 300°F and bake an additional 25 minutes or until filling is set.

1 pie.

TOMATO SOUP CAKE

Darlene Schwab, Orangevale, CA

CAKE

1½ cups sugar

½ cup shortening

1 (26-oz.) can tomato soup

2½ cups all-purpose flour

1 teaspoon baking soda

1 teaspoon baking powder

½ teaspoon ground cloves

½ teaspoon ground nutmeg

1 teaspoon ground cinnamon

Dash salt

½ cup raisins

1 cup chopped walnuts

FROSTING

1 (3-oz.) pkg. cream cheese, softened

¼ cup butter, softened

1 teaspoon vanilla extract

2 cups sifted powdered sugar

Chopped nuts, if desired

1 For Cake: Heat oven to 350°F. Grease and flour 13 x 9-inch baking pan. In large bowl, mix together sugar, shortening, tomato soup, flour, baking soda, baking powder, cloves, nutmeg, cinnamon, salt, raisins and walnuts. Pour mixture into prepared pan. Bake 25 minutes; cool completely.

2 For Frosting: In large bowl, beat together cream cheese, butter and vanilla until light and fluffy. Gradually add powdered sugar. Beat until smooth. Spread on cooled cake. Sprinkle with extra chopped nuts, if desired.

10 to 12 servings.

GINGERBREAD, PEAR, MANDARIN ORANGE UPSIDE-DOWN CAKE

Sharon Sheets, Rio Dell, CA

FRUIT TOPPING

2 tablespoons butter

½ cup packed dark brown sugar

1 teaspoon dark molasses

1 (15-oz.) can sliced pears, drained, reserving 1 tablespoon syrup or fresh pears, thinly sliced

1 small can mandarin oranges, drained, reserving 1 tablespoon syrup

CAKE

1½ cups all-purpose flour

¾ teaspoon ground cinnamon

¾ teaspoon ground ginger

2 teaspoons baking powder

½ teaspoon baking soda

½ cup butter, softened

¼ cup packed brown sugar

1 egg, room temperature

1 cup dark molasses

½ teaspoon orange extract, if desired

½ cup water

❶ For Fruit Topping: Melt butter in an 8- or 9-inch round glass dish with 2-inch-high edges in oven. Remove and stir in brown sugar, molasses and syrup from fruits. Stir until well blended. Arrange pears and orange slices alternately in pan. Set aside.

❷ For Cake: Heat oven to 350°F. In small bowl, combine flour, cinnamon, ginger, baking powder and baking soda until well blended. In large bowl, cream butter and brown sugar until fluffy. Add egg and molasses and beat until fluffy. Add orange extract to water. Alternately add flour and water, blending slowly after each addition. Using large spoon, gently place cake over fruit topping. Bake 35 to 40 minutes or until toothpick inserted in center comes out clean; cool 5 minutes. Loosen edges of cake and carefully invert onto platter. Cool 20 to 30 minutes and top with whipped cream or whipped topping. Serve warm or cold.

8 to 10 servings.

Gingerbread, Pear, Mandarin Orange Upside-Down Cake

BLUEBERRY MUFFINS

Dorothy Anderson, Sacramento, CA

½ cup butter

¼ cup sugar

2 eggs, beaten

½ cup cream

5 tablespoons milk

½ teaspoon vanilla extract

2 cups cake flour

2 teaspoons baking powder

¼ teaspoon salt

½ cup well-drained canned or fresh blueberries

1 Heat oven to 350°F.

2 Cream butter in large bowl. Add sugar, a small amount at a time, and blend well. Add eggs; beat mixture 3 minutes. Combine cream, milk and vanilla in small bowl. Sift together flour, baking powder and salt in medium bowl. Stir in with wooden spoon about one third at a time, alternately with milk mixture. Gently fold in blueberries. Line 12 muffin pans with paper liners and fill half full. Bake 20 to 30 minutes or until light golden brown and top springs back when pressed lightly. Cool on wire rack.

12 servings.

BLUEBERRY ORANGE BREAD

Hope Wasylenki, Gahanna, OH

BREAD

2 tablespoons butter

¼ cup boiling water

½ cup orange juice

3 teaspoons grated orange peel

1 egg

1 cup sugar

2 cups all-purpose flour

1 teaspoon baking powder

¼ teaspoon baking soda

½ teaspoon salt

1 cup fresh or thawed frozen blueberries

GLAZE

2 tablespoons orange juice

1 teaspoon grated orange peel

2 tablespoons honey

1 For Bread: Heat oven to 325°F. Grease 9x5 or 1½-quart loaf pan. Melt butter in boiling water in small pan. Stir in juice and orange peel. Beat egg and sugar until light and fluffy in medium bowl. Sift together sugar, flour, baking powder, baking soda and salt in medium bowl. Add sifted dry ingredients alternately with orange liquid, beating until smooth. Fold in blueberries. Bake 60 to 70 minutes or until toothpick inserted in center comes out clean; cool slightly and turn out onto platter.

2 For Glaze: In small bowl, stir together orange juice, orange peel and honey. Spoon glaze over hot bread; cool completely.

10 to 12 servings.

CRANBERRY BREAD

Lissa Carrino, Medina, OH

2 cups all-purpose flour

¾ cup sugar

1½ teaspoons baking powder

¾ teaspoon salt

½ teaspoon baking soda

¼ cup butter, softened

1 tablespoon grated orange peel

¾ cup orange juice

1 egg

1 cup cranberries, halved

½ cup chopped walnuts

1 Heat oven to 350°F. Grease bottom of loaf pan.

2 In large bowl, mix flour, sugar, baking powder, salt and baking soda. Stir in butter until crumbly. Stir in orange peel, juice and egg until just moistened. Stir in cranberries and nuts. Pour into prepared pan and bake 1 hour or until toothpick inserted in center comes out clean.

10 to 12 servings.

BEN'S TANTALIZINGLY TANGY AND TASTY CHERRY CREAM PIE

Ben R. Bessent, Norfolk, VA

⅔ cup lemon or lime juice

2 (14-oz.) cans sweetened condensed milk

1 cup heavy whipping cream, whipped to soft peak

2 cans red tart pitted cherries, drained, chilled

1 cup chopped pecans

2 (9-inch) graham-cracker pie shells

1 In medium bowl stir lemon juice into condensed milk until mixture thickens; fold in whipped cream. Fold in cherries and pecans gently until thoroughly blended. Fill pie shells. Cover and refrigerate at least 8 hours or overnight.

2 pies.

GOAT'S MILK RICE PUDDING

Tom Hunt, Blairsville, PA

5 cups goat's milk

⅔ cup arborio rice

½ cup sugar

2 teaspoons vanilla extract

2 teaspoons dark rum

1 teaspoon grated orange peel

Cinnamon

Whipped cream

Maraschino cherries

1 Place milk and rice in heavy-bottomed, medium saucepan. Bring to a boil; reduce heat and simmer 25 minutes. Stir in sugar, vanilla, dark rum and orange peel. Cook 10 minutes or until rice is tender. Spoon into dessert bowls and sprinkle with cinnamon; cover with plastic wrap. Cool in refrigerator at least 2 hours. Serve with a dollop of whipped cream and top with a maraschino cherry.

4 to 6 servings.

CHOCOLATE TOWN PIE

Angelana Cristan, Marquette, MI

1 (9-inch) pie crust

8 tablespoons butter

2 eggs

½ cup all-purpose flour

8 oz. chocolate chips

½ cup chopped nuts

1 Heat oven to 350°F. Prepare pie crust using 9-inch pie pan.

2 In large bowl mix together butter, eggs, flour, chocolate chips and nuts. Pour mixture into prepared pie crust. Bake until crust is golden brown and filling is set.

1 pie.

RECIPE INDEX

GENERAL INDEX